ROALD DAHL was a spy, ace fighter pilot, chocolate historian and medical inventor. He was also the author of *Charlie and the Chocolate Factory*, *Matilda*, *The BFG* and many more brilliant stories. He remains **THE WORLD'S NUMBER ONE STORYTELLER.**

QUENTIN BLAKE has illustrated more than three hundred books and was Roald Dahl's favourite illustrator. In 1980 he won the prestigious Kate Greenaway Medal. In 1999 he became the first ever Children's Laureate and in 2013 he was knighted for services to illustration.

Books by Roald Dahl

THE BFG
BOY: TALES OF CHILDHOOD
BOY *and* GOING SOLO
CHARLIE AND THE CHOCOLATE FACTORY
CHARLIE AND THE GREAT GLASS ELEVATOR
THE COMPLETE ADVENTURES OF CHARLIE AND MR WILLY WONKA
DANNY THE CHAMPION OF THE WORLD
THE ENORMOUS CROCODILE
ESIO TROT
FANTASTIC MR FOX
GEORGE'S MARVELLOUS MEDICINE
THE GIRAFFE AND THE PELLY AND ME
GOING SOLO
JAMES AND THE GIANT PEACH
MATILDA
THE MAGIC FINGER
THE TWITS
THE WITCHES

Picture books

DIRTY BEASTS
THE ENORMOUS CROCODILE
THE GIRAFFE AND THE PELLY AND ME
THE MINPINS
REVOLTING RHYMES

Plays

THE BFG: PLAYS FOR CHILDREN (*Adapted by David Wood*)
CHARLIE AND THE CHOCOLATE FACTORY: A PLAY (*Adapted by Richard George*)
DANNY THE CHAMPION OF THE WORLD: PLAYS FOR CHILDREN
(*Adapted by David Wood*)
FANTASTIC MR FOX: A PLAY (*Adapted by Sally Reid*)
JAMES AND THE GIANT PEACH: A PLAY (*Adapted by Richard George*)
THE TWITS: PLAYS FOR CHILDREN (*Adapted by David Wood*)
THE WITCHES: PLAYS FOR CHILDREN (*Adapted by David Wood*)

Teenage fiction

THE GREAT AUTOMATIC GRAMMATIZATOR AND OTHER STORIES
RHYME STEW
SKIN AND OTHER STORIES
THE VICAR OF NIBBLESWICKE
THE WONDERFUL STORY OF HENRY SUGAR AND SIX MORE

Collections

THE ROALD DAHL TREASURY
SONGS AND VERSE

ROALD DAHL

BOY

Illustrated by **Quentin Blake**

PUFFIN

Find out more about Roald Dahl
by visiting the website at
roalddahl.com

PUFFIN BOOKS

UK | USA | Canada | Ireland | Australia
India | New Zealand | South Africa

Puffin Books is part of the Penguin Random House group of companies
whose addresses can be found at global.penguinrandomhouse.com.

puffinbooks.com

Penguin
Random House
UK

First published in Great Britain by Jonathan Cape
and in the USA by Farrar, Straus and Giroux 1984
Published by Puffin Books 1986
Published with new artwork 2013
This edition published 2016
012

Text and archive photographs copyright © Roald Dahl Nominee Ltd, 1984
Illustrations copyright © Quentin Blake, 2013
The moral right of Roald Dahl and Quentin Blake has been asserted

Set in Bembo 13/15pt by
Palimpsest Book Production Limited, Falkirk, Stirlingshire
Printed in Great Britain by Clays Ltd, St Ives plc

A CIP catalogue record for this book is available from the British Library

ISBN: 978-0-141-36553-4

www.greenpenguin.co.uk

For
Alfhild, Else, Asta,
Ellen and Louis

Contents

An autobiography is a book a person writes about his own life and it is usually full of all sorts of boring details.

This is not an autobiography. I would never write a history of myself. On the other hand, throughout my young days at school and just afterwards a number of things happened to me that I have never forgotten.

None of these things is important, but each of them made such a tremendous impression on me that I have never been able to get them out of my mind. Each of them, even after a lapse of fifty and sometimes sixty years, has remained seared on my memory.

I didn't have to search for any of them. All I had to do was skim them off the top of my consciousness and write them down.

Some are funny. Some are painful. Some are unpleasant. I suppose that is why I have always remembered them so vividly. All are true.

R. D.

Starting-point

Wendy House

Alfhild Ellen and Else me and Astri
Radyr

Papa and Mama

My father, Harald Dahl, was a Norwegian who came from a small town near Oslo, called Sarpsborg. His own father, my grandfather, was a fairly prosperous merchant who owned a store in Sarpsborg and traded in just about everything from cheese to chicken-wire.

I am writing these words in 1984, but this grandfather of mine was born, believe it or not, in 1820, shortly after Wellington had defeated Napoleon at Waterloo. If my grandfather had been alive today he would have been one hundred and sixty-four years old. My father would have been one hundred and twenty-one. Both my father and my grandfather were late starters so far as children were concerned.

When my father was fourteen, which is still more than one hundred years ago, he was up on the roof of the family house replacing some loose tiles when he slipped and fell. He broke his left arm below the elbow. Somebody ran to fetch the doctor, and half an hour later this gentleman made a majestic and drunken arrival in his horse-drawn buggy. He was so drunk that he mistook the fractured elbow for a dislocated elbow.

'We'll soon put this back into place!' he cried out, and two men were called off the street to help with the pulling. They were instructed to hold my father by the waist while the doctor grabbed him by the wrist of the broken arm and shouted, 'Pull men, pull! Pull as hard as you can!'

The pain must have been excruciating. The victim screamed, and his mother, who was watching the performance in horror, shouted 'Stop!' But by then the pullers had done so much damage that a splinter of bone was sticking out through the skin of the forearm.

 This was in 1877 and orthopaedic surgery was not what it is today. So they simply amputated the arm at the elbow, and for the rest of his life my father had to manage with one arm. Fortunately, it was the left arm that he lost and gradually, over the years, he taught himself to do more or less anything he wanted with just the four fingers and thumb of his right hand. He could tie a shoelace as quickly as you or me, and for cutting up the food on his plate, he sharpened the bottom edge of a fork so that it served as both knife and fork all in one. He kept his ingenious instrument in a slim leather case and carried it in his pocket wherever he went. The loss of an arm, he used to say, caused him only one serious inconvenience. He found it impossible to cut the top off a boiled egg.

My father was a year or so older than his brother Oscar, but they were exceptionally close, and soon after they left school, they went for a long walk together to plan their future. They decided that a small town like Sarpsborg in a small country like Norway was no place in which to make a fortune. So what they must do, they agreed, was go away to one of the big countries, either to England or France, where opportunities to make good would be boundless.

Their own father, an amiable giant nearly seven foot tall, lacked the drive and ambition of his sons, and he refused to support this tomfool idea. When he forbade them to go, they ran away from home, and somehow or other the two of them managed to work their way to France on a cargo ship.

From Calais they went to Paris, and in Paris they agreed to separate because each of them wished to be independent of the other. Uncle Oscar, for some reason, headed west for La Rochelle on the Atlantic coast, while my father remained in Paris for the time being.

The story of how these two brothers each started a totally separate business in different countries and how each of them made a fortune is interesting, but there is no time to tell it here except in the briefest manner.

Take my Uncle Oscar first. La Rochelle was then, and still is, a fishing port. By the time he was forty he had become the wealthiest man in town. He owned a fleet of trawlers called 'Pêcheurs d'Atlantique' and a large canning factory to can the sardines his trawlers brought in. He acquired a wife from a good family and a magnificent town house as well as a large château in the country. He became a collector of Louis XV furniture, good pictures and rare books, and all these beautiful things together with the two properties are still in the family. I have not seen the château in the country, but I was in the La Rochelle house a couple of years ago and it really is something. The furniture alone should be in a museum.

While Uncle Oscar was bustling around in La Rochelle, his one-armed brother Harald (my own father) was not sitting on his rump doing nothing. He had met in Paris another young Norwegian called Aadnesen and the two of them now decided to form a partnership and become shipbrokers. A shipbroker is a person who supplies a ship with everything it needs when it comes into port – fuel and food, ropes and paint, soap and towels, hammers and nails, and thousands of other tiddly little items. A shipbroker is a kind of enormous shopkeeper for ships, and by far the most important item he supplies to them is the fuel on which the ship's engines run. In those days fuel meant only one thing. It meant coal. There were no oil-burning motorships on the high seas at that time. All ships were steamships and these old steamers would take on hundreds and often thousands of tons of coal in one go. To the shipbrokers, coal was black gold.

Paint   Rope   Soap

My father and his new-found friend, Mr Aadnesen, understood all this very well. It made sense, they told each other, to set up their shipbroking business in one of the great coaling ports of Europe. Which was it to be? The answer was simple. The greatest coaling port in the world at that time was Cardiff, in South Wales. So off to Cardiff they went, these two ambitious young men, carrying with them little or no luggage. But my father had something more delightful than luggage. He had a wife, a young French girl called Marie whom he had recently married in Paris.

In Cardiff, the shipbroking firm of 'Aadnesen & Dahl' was set up and a single room in Bute Street was rented as an office. From then on, we have what sounds like one of those exaggerated fairy-stories of success, but in reality it was the result of tremendous hard and brainy work by those two friends. Very soon 'Aadnesen & Dahl' had more business than the partners could handle alone. Larger office space was acquired and more staff were engaged. The real money then began rolling in. Within a few years, my father was able to buy a fine house in the village of Llandaff, just outside Cardiff, and there his wife Marie bore him two children, a girl and a boy. But tragically, she died after giving birth to the second child.

When the shock and sorrow of her death had begun to subside a little, my father suddenly realized that his two small children ought at the very least to have a stepmother to care for them. What is more, he felt terribly lonely. It was quite obvious that he must try to find himself another wife. But this was easier said than done for a Norwegian living in South Wales who didn't know very many people. So he decided to take a holiday and travel back to his own country, Norway, and who knows, he might if he was lucky find himself a lovely new bride in his own country.

Over in Norway, during the summer of 1911, while taking a trip in a small coastal steamer in the Oslofjord, he met a young lady called Sofie Magdalene Hesselberg. Being a fellow who knew a good thing when he saw one, he proposed to her within a week and married her soon after that.

Mama Engaged

Harald Dahl took his Norwegian wife on a honeymoon in Paris, and after that back to the house in Llandaff. The two of them were

me at 8 months

deeply in love and blissfully happy, and during the next six years she bore him four children, a girl, another girl, a boy (me) and a third girl. There were now six children in the family, two by my father's first wife and four by his second. A larger and grander house was needed and the money was there to buy it.

the house at Radyr

So in 1918, when I was two, we all moved into an imposing country mansion beside the village of Radyr, about eight miles west of Cardiff. I remember it as a mighty house with turrets on its roof and with majestic lawns and terraces all around it. There were many acres of farm and woodland, and a number of cottages for the staff. Very soon, the meadows were full of milking cows and the sties were full of pigs and the chicken-run was full of chickens. There were several massive shire-horses for pulling the ploughs and the hay-wagons, and there was a ploughman and a cowman and a couple of gardeners and all manner of servants in the house itself. Like his brother Oscar in La Rochelle, Harald Dahl had made it in no uncertain manner.

But what interests me most of all about these two brothers, Harald and Oscar, is this. Although they came from a simple unsophisticated small-town family, both of them, quite independently of one another, developed a powerful interest in beautiful things. As soon as they could afford it, they began to fill their houses with lovely paintings and fine furniture. In addition to that, my father became an expert gardener and above all a collector of alpine plants. My mother used to tell me how the two of them would go on expeditions up into the mountains of Norway and how he would frighten her to death by climbing one-handed up steep cliff-faces to reach small alpine plants growing high up on some rocky ledge. He was also an accomplished wood-carver, and most of the mirror-frames in the house were his own work. So indeed was the entire mantelpiece around the fireplace in the living-room, a splendid design of fruit and foliage and inter-twining branches carved in oak.

He was a tremendous diary-writer. I still have one of his many notebooks from the Great War of 1914–18. Every single day during those five war years he would write several pages of comment and observation about the events of the time. He wrote with a pen and although Norwegian was his mother-tongue, he always wrote his diaries in perfect English.

He harboured a curious theory about how to develop a sense of beauty in the minds of his children. Every time my mother became pregnant, he would wait until the last three months of her pregnancy, and then he would announce to her that 'the glorious walks' must begin. These glorious walks consisted of him taking her to places of great beauty in the countryside and walking with her for about an hour each day so that she could absorb the splendour of the surroundings. His theory was that if the eye of a pregnant woman was constantly observing the beauty of nature, this beauty would somehow become transmitted to the mind of the unborn baby within her womb and that baby would grow up to be a lover of beautiful things. This was the treatment that all of his children received before they were born.

a letter from Papa

Kindergarten, 1922–3 (age 6–7)

In 1920, when I was still only three, my mother's eldest child, my own sister Astri, died from appendicitis. She was seven years old when she died, which was also the age of my own eldest daughter, Olivia, when she died from measles forty-two years later.

Astri was far and away my father's favourite. He adored her beyond measure and her sudden death left him literally speechless for days afterwards. He was so overwhelmed with grief that when he himself went down with pneumonia a month or so afterwards, he did not much care whether he lived or died.

If they had had penicillin in those days, neither appendicitis nor pneumonia would have been so much of a threat, but with no penicillin or any other magical antibiotic cures, pneumonia in particular was a very dangerous illness indeed. The pneumonia patient, on about the fourth or fifth day, would invariably reach what was known as 'the crisis'. The temperature soared and the pulse became rapid. The patient had to fight to survive. My father refused to fight. He was thinking, I am quite sure, of his beloved daughter, and he was wanting to join her in heaven. So he died. He was fifty-seven years old.

My mother had now lost a daughter and a husband all in the space of a few weeks. Heaven knows what it must have felt like to be hit with a double catastrophe like this. Here she was, a young Norwegian in a foreign land, suddenly having to face all alone the very gravest problems and responsibilities. She had five children to look after, three of her own and two by her husband's first wife, and to make matters worse, she herself was expecting another baby in two months' time. A less courageous woman would almost certainly have sold the house and packed her bags and headed straight back to Norway with the children. Over there in her own country she had her mother and father willing and waiting to help her, as well as her two unmarried sisters. But she refused to take the easy way out. Her husband had always stated most emphatically that he wished all his children to be educated in English schools. They were the best in the world, he used to say. Better by far than the Norwegian ones. Better even than the Welsh ones, despite the fact that he lived in Wales and had his business there.

He maintained that there was some kind of magic about English schooling and that the education it provided had caused the inhabitants of a small island to become a great nation and a great Empire and to produce the world's greatest literature. 'No child of mine,' he kept saying, 'is going to school anywhere else but in England.' My mother was determined to carry out the wishes of her dead husband.

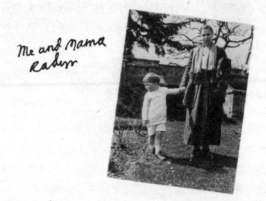

Me and Mama
Radyr

To accomplish this, she would have to move house from Wales to England, but she wasn't ready for that yet. She must stay here in Wales for a while longer, where she knew people who could help and advise her, especially her husband's great friend and partner, Mr Aadnesen. But even if she wasn't leaving Wales quite yet, it was essential that she move to a smaller and more manageable house. She had enough children to look after without having to bother about a farm as well. So as soon as her fifth child (another daughter) was born, she sold the big house and moved to a smaller one a few miles away in Llandaff. It was called Cumberland Lodge and it was nothing more than a pleasant medium-sized suburban villa. So it was in Llandaff two years later, when I was six years old, that I went to my first school.

Me, six

The school was a kindergarten run by two sisters, Mrs Corfield and Miss Tucker, and it was called Elmtree House. It is astonishing how little one remembers about one's life before the age of seven or eight. I can tell you all sorts of things that happened to me from eight onwards, but only very few before that. I went for a whole year to Elmtree House but I cannot even remember what my classroom looked like. Nor can I picture the faces of Mrs Corfield or Miss Tucker, although I am sure they were sweet and smiling. I do have a blurred memory of sitting on the stairs and trying over and over again to tie one of my shoelaces, but that is all that comes back to me at this distance of the school itself.

On the other hand, I can remember very clearly the journeys I made to and from the school because they were so tremendously exciting. Great excitement is probably the only thing that really interests a six-year-old boy and it sticks in his mind. In my case, the excitement centred around my new tricycle. I rode to school on it every day with my eldest sister riding on hers. No grown-ups came with us, and I can remember oh so vividly how the two of us used to go racing at enormous tricycle speeds down the middle of the road and then, most glorious of all, when we came to a corner, we would lean to one side and take it on two wheels. All this, you must realize, was in the good old days when the sight of a motor-car on the street was an event, and it was quite safe for tiny children to go tricycling and whooping their way to school in the centre of the highway.

So much, then, for my memories of kindergarten sixty-two years ago. It's not much, but it's all there is left.

Llandaff
Cathedral School,
1923–5
(age 7–9)

Else, me, Alfhild

A picnic with Mama

The Bicycle and the Sweet-shop

When I was seven, my mother decided I should leave kindergarten and go to a proper boys' school. By good fortune, there existed a well-known Preparatory School for boys about a mile from our house. It was called Llandaff Cathedral School, and it stood right under the shadow of Llandaff cathedral. Like the cathedral, the school is still there and still flourishing.

Llandaff Cathedral

But here again, I can remember very little about the two years I attended Llandaff Cathedral School, between the age of seven and nine. Only two moments remain clearly in my mind. The first lasted not more than five seconds but I will never forget it.

It was my first term and I was walking home alone across the village green after school when suddenly one of the senior twelve-year-old boys came riding full speed down the road on his bicycle about twenty yards away from me. The road was on a hill and the boy was going down the slope, and as he flashed by he started backpedalling very quickly so that the free-wheeling mechanism of his bike made a loud whirring sound. At the same time, he took his hands off the handlebars and folded them casually across his chest. I stopped dead and stared after him. How wonderful he was! How swift and brave and graceful in his long trousers with bicycle-clips around them and his scarlet school cap at a jaunty angle on his head! One day, I told myself, one glorious day I will have a bike like that and I will wear long trousers with bicycle-clips and my school cap will sit jaunty on my head and I will go whizzing down the hill pedalling backwards with no hands on the handlebars!

I promise you that if somebody had caught me by the shoulder at that moment and said to me, 'What is your greatest wish in life, little boy? What is your absolute ambition? To be a doctor? A fine musician? A painter? A writer? Or the Lord Chancellor?' I would have answered without hesitation that my only ambition, my hope, my longing was to have a bike like that and to go whizzing down the hill with no hands on the handlebars. It would be fabulous. It made me tremble just to think about it.

My second and only other memory of Llandaff Cathedral School is extremely bizarre. It happened a little over a year later, when I was just nine. By then I had made some friends and when I walked to school in the mornings I would start out alone but would pick up four other boys of my own age along the way. After school was over, the same four boys and I would set out together across the village green and through the village itself, heading for home. On the way to school and on the way back we always passed the sweet-shop. No we didn't, we never passed it. We always stopped. We lingered outside its rather small window gazing in at the big glass jars full of Bull's-eyes and Old Fashioned Humbugs and Strawberry Bonbons and Glacier Mints and Acid Drops and Pear Drops and Lemon Drops and all the rest of them. Each of us received sixpence a week for pocket-money, and whenever there was any money in our pockets, we would all troop in together to buy a pennyworth of this or that. My own favourites were Sherbet Suckers and Liquorice Bootlaces.

One of the other boys, whose name was Thwaites, told me I should never eat Liquorice Bootlaces. Thwaites's father, who was a doctor, had said that they were made from rats' blood. The father had given his young son a lecture about Liquorice Bootlaces when he had caught him eating one in bed. 'Every ratcatcher in the country,' the father had said, 'takes his rats to the Liquorice Bootlace Factory, and the manager pays tuppence for each rat. Many a ratcatcher has become a millionaire by selling his dead rats to the Factory.'

'But how do they turn the rats into liquorice?' the young Thwaites had asked his father.

'They wait until they've got ten thousand rats,' the father had answered, 'then they dump them all into a huge shiny steel cauldron and boil them up for several hours. Two men stir the bubbling cauldron with long poles and in the end they have a thick steaming rat-stew. After that, a cruncher is lowered into the cauldron to crunch the bones, and what's left is a pulpy substance called rat-mash.'

'Yes, but how do they turn that into Liquorice Bootlaces, Daddy?' the young Thwaites had asked, and this question, according to Thwaites, had caused his father to pause and think for a few moments before he answered it. At last he had said, 'The two men who were doing the stirring with the long poles now put on their wellington boots and climb into the cauldron and shovel the hot rat-mash out on to a concrete floor. Then they run a steam-roller over it several times to flatten it out. What is left looks rather like a gigantic black pancake, and all they have to do after that is to wait for it to cool and to harden so they can cut it up into strips to make the Bootlaces. Don't ever eat them,' the father had said. 'If you do, you'll get ratitis.'

'What is ratitis, Daddy?' young Thwaites had asked.

'All the rats that the rat-catchers catch are poisoned with rat-poison,' the father had said. 'It's the rat-poison that gives you ratitis.'

'Yes, but what happens to you when you catch it?' young Thwaites had asked.

'Your teeth become very sharp and pointed,' the father had answered. 'And a short stumpy tail grows out of your back just above your bottom. There is no cure for ratitis. I ought to know. I'm a doctor.'

We all enjoyed Thwaites's story and we made him tell it to us many times on our walks to and from school. But it didn't stop any of us except Thwaites from buying Liquorice Bootlaces. At two for a penny they were the best value in the shop. A Bootlace, in case you haven't had the pleasure of handling one, is not round. It's like a flat black tape about half an inch wide. You buy it rolled up in a coil, and in those days it used to be so long that when you unrolled it and held one end at arm's length above your head, the other end touched the ground.

Sherbet Suckers were also two a penny. Each Sucker consisted of a yellow cardboard tube filled with sherbet powder, and there was a hollow liquorice straw sticking out of it. (Rat's blood again, young Thwaites would warn us, pointing at the liquorice straw.) You sucked the sherbet up through the straw and when it was finished you ate the liquorice. They were delicious, those Sherbet Suckers. The sherbet fizzed in your mouth, and if you knew how to do it, you could make white froth come out of your nostrils and pretend you were throwing a fit.

Gobstoppers, costing a penny each, were enormous hard round balls the size of small tomatoes. One Gobstopper would provide about an hour's worth of non-stop sucking and if you took it out of your mouth and inspected it every five minutes or so, you would find it had changed colour. There was something fascinating about the way it went from pink to blue to green to yellow. We used to wonder how in the world the Gobstopper Factory managed to achieve this magic. 'How *does* it happen?' we would ask each other. 'How *can* they make it keep changing colour?'

'It's your spit that does it,' young Thwaites proclaimed. As the son of a doctor, he considered himself to be an authority on all things that had to do with the body. He could tell us about scabs and when they were ready to be picked off. He knew why a black eye was blue and why blood was red. 'It's your spit that makes a Gobstopper change colour,' he kept insisting. When we asked him to elaborate on this theory, he answered, 'You wouldn't understand it if I did tell you.'

Pear Drops were exciting because they had a dangerous taste. They smelled of nail-varnish and they froze the back of your throat. All of us were warned against eating them, and the result was that we ate them more than ever.

Then there was a hard brown lozenge called the Tonsil Tickler. The Tonsil Tickler tasted and smelled very strongly of chloroform. We had not the slightest doubt that these things were saturated in the dreaded anaesthetic which, as Thwaites had many times pointed out to us, could put you to sleep for hours at a stretch. 'If my father has to saw off somebody's leg,' he said, 'he pours chloroform on to a pad and the person sniffs it and goes to sleep and my father saws his leg off without him even feeling it.'

'But why do they put it into sweets and sell them to us?' we asked him.

You might think a question like this would have baffled Thwaites. But Thwaites was never baffled. 'My father says Tonsil Ticklers were invented for dangerous prisoners in jail,' he said. 'They give them one with each meal and the chloroform makes them sleepy and stops them rioting.'

'Yes,' we said, 'but why sell them to children?'

'It's a plot,' Thwaites said. 'A grown-up plot to keep us quiet.'

The sweet-shop in Llandaff in the year 1923 was the very centre of our lives. To us, it was what a bar is to a drunk, or a church is to a Bishop. Without it, there would have been little to live for. But it had one terrible drawback, this sweet-shop. The woman who owned it was a horror. We hated her and we had good reason for doing so.

Her name was Mrs Pratchett. She was a small skinny old hag with a moustache on her upper lip and a mouth as sour as a green gooseberry. She never smiled. She never welcomed us when we went in, and the only times she spoke were when she said things like, 'I'm watchin' you so keep yer thievin' fingers off them chocolates!' Or 'I don't want you in 'ere just to look around! Either you *forks* out or you *gets* out!'

But by far the most loathsome thing about Mrs Pratchett was the filth that clung around her. Her apron was grey and greasy. Her blouse had bits of breakfast all over it, toast-crumbs and tea stains and splotches of dried egg-yolk. It was her hands, however, that disturbed us most. They were disgusting. They were black with dirt and grime. They looked as though they had been putting lumps of coal on the fire all day long. And do not forget please that it was these very hands and fingers that she plunged into the sweet-jars when we asked for a pennyworth of Treacle Toffee or Wine Gums or Nut Clusters or whatever. There were precious few health laws in those days, and nobody, least of all Mrs Pratchett, ever thought of using a little shovel for getting out the sweets as they do today. The mere sight of her grimy right hand with its black fingernails digging an ounce of Chocolate Fudge out of a jar would have caused a starving tramp to go running from the shop. But not us. Sweets were our life-blood. We would have put up with far worse than that to get them. So we simply stood and watched in sullen silence while this disgusting old woman stirred around inside the jars with her foul fingers.

The other thing we hated Mrs Pratchett for was her meanness. Unless you spent a whole sixpence all in one go, she wouldn't give you a bag. Instead you got your sweets twisted up in a small piece of newspaper which she tore off a pile of old *Daily Mirrors* lying on the counter.

So you can well understand that we had it in for Mrs Pratchett in a big way, but we didn't quite know what to do about it. Many schemes were put forward but none of them was any good. None of them, that is, until suddenly, one memorable afternoon, we found the dead mouse.

The Great Mouse Plot

My four friends and I had come across a loose floor-board at the back of the classroom, and when we prised it up with the blade of a pocket-knife, we discovered a big hollow space underneath. This, we decided, would be our secret hiding place for sweets and other small treasures such as conkers and monkey-nuts and birds' eggs. Every afternoon, when the last lesson was over, the five of us would wait until the classroom had emptied, then we would lift up the floor-board and examine our secret hoard, perhaps adding to it or taking something away.

One day, when we lifted it up, we found a dead mouse lying among our treasures. It was an exciting discovery. Thwaites took it out by its tail and waved it in front of our faces. 'What shall we do with it?' he cried.

'It stinks!' someone shouted. 'Throw it out of the window quick!'

'Hold on a tick,' I said. 'Don't throw it away.'

Thwaites hesitated. They all looked at me.

When writing about oneself, one must strive to be truthful. Truth is more important than modesty. I must tell you, therefore, that it was I and I alone who had the idea for the great and daring Mouse Plot. We all have our moments of brilliance and glory, and this was mine.

'Why don't we,' I said, 'slip it into one of Mrs Pratchett's jars of sweets? Then when she puts her dirty hand in to grab a handful, she'll grab a stinky dead mouse instead.'

The other four stared at me in wonder. Then, as the sheer genius of the plot began to sink in, they all started grinning. They slapped me on the back. They cheered me and danced around the classroom. 'We'll do it today!' they cried. 'We'll do it on the way home! *You* had the idea,' they said to me, 'so *you* can be the one to put the mouse in the jar.'

Thwaites handed me the mouse. I put it into my trouser pocket. Then the five of us left the school, crossed the village green and headed for the sweet-shop. We were tremendously jazzed up. We felt like a gang of desperadoes setting out to rob a train or blow up the sheriff's office.

'Make sure you put it into a jar which is used often,' somebody said.

'I'm putting it in Gobstoppers,' I said. 'The Gobstopper jar is never behind the counter.'

'I've got a penny,' Thwaites said, 'so I'll ask for one Sherbet Sucker and one Bootlace. And while she turns away to get them, you slip the mouse in quickly with the Gobstoppers.'

Thus everything was arranged. We were strutting a little as we entered the shop. We were the victors now and Mrs Pratchett was the victim. She stood behind the counter, and her small malignant pig-eyes watched us suspiciously as we came forward.

'One Sherbet Sucker, please,' Thwaites said to her, holding out his penny.

I kept to the rear of the group, and when I saw Mrs Pratchett turn her head away for a couple of seconds to fish a Sherbet Sucker out of the box, I lifted the heavy glass lid of the Gobstopper jar and dropped the mouse in. Then I replaced the lid as silently as possible. My heart was thumping like mad and my hands had gone all sweaty.

'And one Bootlace, please,' I heard Thwaites saying. When I turned round, I saw Mrs Pratchett holding out the Bootlace in her filthy fingers.

'I don't want all the lot of you troopin' in 'ere if only one of you is buyin',' she screamed at us. 'Now beat it! Go on, get out!'

As soon as we were outside, we broke into a run. 'Did you do it?' they shouted at me.

'Of course I did!' I said.

'Well done you!' they cried. 'What a super show!'

I felt like a hero. I *was* a hero. It was marvellous to be so popular.

Mr Coombes

The flush of triumph over the dead mouse was carried forward to the next morning as we all met again to walk to school.

'Let's go in and see if it's still in the jar,' somebody said as we approached the sweet-shop.

'Don't,' Thwaites said firmly. 'It's too dangerous. Walk past as though nothing has happened.'

As we came level with the shop we saw a cardboard notice hanging on the door.

We stopped and stared. We had never known the sweet-shop to be closed at this time in the morning, even on Sundays.

'What's happened?' we asked each other. 'What's going on?'

We pressed our faces against the window and looked inside. Mrs Pratchett was nowhere to be seen.

'Look!' I cried. 'The Gobstopper jar's gone! It's not on the shelf! There's a gap where it used to be!'

'It's on the floor!' someone said. 'It's smashed to bits and there's Gobstoppers everywhere!'

'There's the mouse!' someone else shouted.

We could see it all, the huge glass jar smashed to smithereens with the dead mouse lying in the wreckage and hundreds of many-coloured Gobstoppers littering the floor.

'She got such a shock when she grabbed hold of the mouse that she dropped everything,' somebody was saying.

'But why didn't she sweep it all up and open the shop?' I asked.

Nobody answered me.

We turned away and walked towards the school. All of a sudden we had begun to feel slightly uncomfortable. There was something not quite right about the shop being closed. Even Thwaites was unable to offer a reasonable explanation. We became silent. There was faint scent of danger in the air now. Each one of us had caught a whiff of it. Alarm bells were beginning to ring faintly in our ears.

After a while, Thwaites broke the silence. 'She must have got one heck of a shock,' he said. He paused. We all looked at him, wondering what wisdom the great medical authority was going to come out with next.

'After all,' he went on, 'to catch hold of a dead mouse when you're expecting to catch hold of a Gobstopper must be a pretty frightening experience. Don't you agree?'

Nobody answered him.

'Well now,' Thwaites went on, 'when an old person like Mrs Pratchett suddenly gets a very big shock, I suppose you know what happens next?'

'What?' we said. 'What happens?'

'You ask my father,' Thwaites said. 'He'll tell you.'

'You tell us,' we said.

'It gives her a heart attack,' Thwaites announced. 'Her heart stops beating and she's dead in five seconds.'

For a moment or two my own heart stopped beating. Thwaites pointed a finger at me and said darkly, 'I'm afraid you've killed her.'

'*Me?*' I cried. 'Why just *me?*'

'It was *your* idea,' he said. 'And what's more, *you* put the mouse in.'

All of a sudden, I was a murderer.

At exactly that point, we heard the school bell ringing in the distance and we had to gallop the rest of the way so as not to be late for prayers.

Prayers were held in the Assembly Hall. We all perched in rows on wooden benches while the teachers sat up on the platform in armchairs, facing us. The five of us scrambled into our places just as the Headmaster marched in, followed by the rest of the staff.

The Headmaster is the only teacher at Llandaff Cathedral School that I can remember, and for a reason you will soon discover, I can remember him very clearly indeed. His name was Mr Coombes and I have a picture in my mind of a giant of a man with a face like a ham and a mass of rusty-coloured hair that sprouted in a tangle all over the top of his head. All grown-ups appear as giants to small children. But headmasters (and policemen) are the biggest giants of all and acquire a marvellously exaggerated stature. It is possible that Mr Coombes was a perfectly normal being, but in my memory he was a giant, a tweed-suited giant who always wore a black gown over his tweeds and a waistcoat under his jacket.

Mr Coombes now proceeded to mumble through the same old prayers we had every day, but this morning, when the last amen had been spoken, he did not turn and lead his group rapidly out of the Hall as usual. He remained standing before us, and it was clear he had an announcement to make.

'The whole school is to go out and line up around the playground immediately,' he said. 'Leave your books behind. And no talking.'

Mr Coombes was looking grim. His hammy pink face had taken on that dangerous scowl which only appeared when he was extremely cross and somebody was for the high-jump. I sat there small and frightened among the rows and rows of other boys, and to me at that moment the Headmaster, with his black gown draped over his shoulders, was like a judge at a murder trial.

'He's after the killer,' Thwaites whispered to me.

I began to shiver.

'I'll bet the police are here already,' Thwaites went on. 'And the Black Maria's waiting outside.'

As we made our way out to the playground, my whole stomach began to feel as though it was slowly filling up with swirling water. *I am only eight years old*, I told myself. *No little boy of eight has ever murdered anyone. It's not possible.*

Out in the playground on this warm cloudy September morning, the Deputy Headmaster was shouting, 'Line up in forms! Sixth Form over there! Fifth Form next to them! Spread out! Spread out! Get on with it! Stop talking all of you!'

Thwaites and I and my other three friends were in the Second Form, the lowest but one, and we lined up against the red-brick wall of the playground shoulder to shoulder. I can remember that when every boy in the school was in his place, the line stretched right around the four sides of the playground – about one hundred small boys altogether, aged between six and twelve, all of us wearing identical grey shorts and grey blazers and grey stockings and black shoes.

'Stop that *talking*!' shouted the Deputy Head. 'I want absolute silence!'

But why for heaven's sake were we in the playground at all? I wondered. And why were we lined up like this? It had never happened before.

I half-expected to see two policemen come bounding out of the school to grab me by the arms and put handcuffs on my wrists.

A single door led out from the school on to the playground. Suddenly it swung open and through it, like the angel of death, strode Mr Coombes, huge and bulky in his tweed suit and black gown, and beside him, believe it or not, right beside him trotted the tiny figure of Mrs Pratchett herself!

Mrs Pratchett was alive!

The relief was tremendous.

'She's alive!' I whispered to Thwaites standing next to me. 'I didn't kill her!' Thwaites ignored me.

'We'll start over here,' Mr Coombes was saying to Mrs Pratchett. He grasped her by one of her skinny arms and led her over to where the Sixth Form was standing. Then, still keeping hold of her arm, he proceeded to lead her at a brisk walk down the line of boys. It was like someone inspecting the troops.

'What on earth are they doing?' I whispered.

Thwaites didn't answer me. I glanced at him. He had gone rather pale.

'Too big,' I heard Mrs Pratchett saying. 'Much too big. It's none of this lot. Let's 'ave a look at some of them titchy ones.'

Mr Coombes increased his pace. 'We'd better go all the way round,' he said. He seemed in a hurry to get it over with now and I could see Mrs Pratchett's skinny goat's legs trotting to keep up with him. They had already inspected one side of the playground where the Sixth Form and half the Fifth Form were standing. We watched them moving down the second side . . . then the third side.

'Still too big,' I heard Mrs Pratchett croaking. 'Much too big! Smaller than these! Much smaller! Where's them nasty little ones?'

They were coming closer to us now . . . closer and closer.

They were starting on the fourth side . . .

Every boy in our form was watching Mr Coombes and Mrs Pratchett as they came walking down the line towards us.

'Nasty cheeky lot, these little 'uns!' I heard Mrs Pratchett muttering. 'They comes into my shop and they thinks they can do what they damn well likes!'

Mr Coombes made no reply to this.

'They nick things when I ain't lookin',' she went on. 'They put their grubby 'ands all over everything and they've got no manners. I don't mind girls, I never 'ave no trouble with girls, but boys is 'ideous and 'orrible! I don't 'ave to tell *you* that, 'Eadmaster, do I?'

'These are the smaller ones,' Mr Coombes said.

I could see Mrs Pratchett's piggy little eyes staring hard at the face of each boy she passed.

Suddenly she let out a high-pitched yell and pointed a dirty finger straight at Thwaites. 'That's 'im!' she yelled. 'That's one of 'em! I'd know 'im a mile away, the scummy little bounder!'

The entire school turned to look at Thwaites. 'W-what have *I* done?' he stuttered, appealing to Mr Coombes.

'Shut up,' Mr Coombes said.

Mrs Pratchett's eyes flicked over and settled on my own face. I looked down and studied the black asphalt surface of the playground.

''Ere's another of 'em!' I heard her yelling. 'That one there!' She was pointing at me now.

'You're quite sure?' Mr Coombes said.

'Of course I'm sure!' she cried. 'I never forgets a face, least of all when it's as sly as that! 'Ee's one of 'em all right! There was five altogether! Now where's them other three?'

The other three, as I knew very well, were coming up next.

Mrs Pratchett's face was glimmering with venom as her eyes travelled beyond me down the line.

'There they are!' she cried out, stabbing the air with her finger. ''*Im* . . . and '*im* . . . and '*im*! That's the five of 'em all right! We don't need to look no farther than this, 'Eadmaster! They're all 'ere, the nasty dirty little pigs! You've got their names, 'ave you?'

'I've got their names, Mrs Pratchett,' Mr Coombes told her. 'I'm much obliged to you.'

'And I'm much obliged to *you*, 'Eadmaster,' she answered.

As Mr Coombes led her away across the playground, we heard her saying, 'Right in the jar of Gobstoppers it was! A stinkin' dead mouse which I will never forget as long as I live!'

'You have my deepest sympathy,' Mr Coombes was muttering.

'Talk about shocks!' she went on. 'When my fingers caught 'old of that nasty soggy stinkin' dead mouse . . .' Her voice trailed away as Mr Coombes led her quickly through the door into the school building.

Mrs Pratchett's Revenge

Our Form Master came into the classroom with a piece of paper in his hand. 'The following are to report to the Headmaster's study at once,' he said. 'Thwaites ... Dahl ...' And then he read out the other three names which I have forgotten.

The five of us stood up and left the room. We didn't speak as we made our way down the long corridor into the Headmaster's private quarters where the dreaded study was situated. Thwaites knocked on the door.

'Enter!'

We sidled in. The room smelled of leather and tobacco. Mr Coombes was standing in the middle of it, dominating everything, a giant of a man if ever there was one, and in his hands he held a long yellow cane which curved round the top like a walking stick.

the cane

'I don't want any lies,' he said. 'I know very well you did it and you were all in it together. Line up over there against the bookcase.'

We lined up. Thwaites in front and I, for some reason, at the very back. I was last in the line.

'You,' Mr Coombes said, pointing the cane at Thwaites. 'Come over here.'

Thwaites went forward very slowly.

'Bend over,' Mr Coombes said.

Thwaites bent over. Our eyes were riveted on him. We were hypnotized by it all. We knew, of course, that boys got the cane now and again, but we had never heard of anyone being made to watch.

'Tighter, boy, tighter!' Mr Coombes snapped out. 'Touch the ground!'

Thwaites touched the carpet with the tips of his fingers.

Mr Coombes stood back and took up a firm stance with his legs well apart. I thought how small Thwaites's bottom looked and how very tight it was. Mr Coombes had his eyes focused squarely upon it. He raised the cane high above his shoulder, and as he brought it down, it made a loud swishing sound, and then there was a crack like a pistol shot as it struck Thwaites's bottom.

Little Thwaites seemed to lift about a foot into the air and he yelled 'Ow-w-w-w-w-w-w-w-w-w!' and straightened up like elastic.

'*'Arder!*' shrieked a voice from over in the corner.

Now it was our turn to jump. We looked round and there, sitting in one of Mr Coombes's big leather armchairs, was the tiny loathsome figure of Mrs Pratchett! She was bounding up and down with excitement. 'Lay it into 'im!' she was shrieking. 'Let 'im 'ave it! Teach 'im a lesson!'

'Get down, boy!' Mr Coombes ordered. 'And stay down! You get an extra one every time you straighten up!'

'That's tellin' 'im!' shrieked Mrs Pratchett. 'That's tellin' the little blighter!'

I could hardly believe what I was seeing. It was like some awful pantomime. The violence was bad enough, and being made to watch it was even worse, but with Mrs Pratchett in the audience the whole thing became a nightmare.

Swish-crack! went the cane.

'Ow-w-w-w-w!' yelled Thwaites.

''Arder!' shrieked Mrs Pratchett. 'Stitch 'im up! Make it sting! Tickle 'im up good and proper! Warm 'is backside for 'im! Go on, warm it up, 'Eadmaster!'

Thwaites received four strokes, and by gum, they were four real whoppers.

'Next!' snapped Mr Coombes.

Thwaites came hopping past us on his toes, clutching his bottom with both hands and yelling, 'Ow! Ouch! Ouch! Ouch! Owwwww!'

With tremendous reluctance, the next boy

sidled forward to his fate. I stood there wishing I hadn't been last in the line. The watching and waiting were probably even greater torture than the event itself.

Mr Coombes's performance the second time was the same as the first. So was Mrs Pratchett's. She kept up her screeching all the way through, exhorting Mr Coombes to greater and still greater efforts, and the awful thing was that he seemed to be responding to her cries. He was like an athlete who is spurred on by the shouts of the crowd in the stands. Whether this was true or not, I was sure of one thing. He wasn't weakening.

My own turn came at last. My mind was swimming and my eyes had gone all blurry as I went forward to bend over. I can remember wishing my mother would suddenly come bursting into the room shouting, 'Stop! How dare you do that to my son!' But she didn't. All I heard was Mrs Pratchett's dreadful high-pitched voice behind me screeching, 'This one's the cheekiest of the bloomin' lot, 'Eadmaster! Make sure you let 'im 'ave it good and strong!'

Mr Coombes did just that. As the first stroke landed and the pistol-crack sounded, I was thrown forward so violently that if my fingers hadn't been touching the carpet, I think I would have fallen flat on my face. As it was, I was able to catch myself on the palms of my hands and keep my balance. At first I heard only the *crack* and felt absolutely nothing at all, but a fraction of a second later the burning sting that flooded across my buttocks was so terrific that all I could do was gasp. I gave a great gushing gasp that emptied my lungs of every breath of air that was in them.

It felt, I promise you, as though someone had laid a red-hot poker against my flesh and was pressing down on it hard.

The second stroke was worse than the first and this was probably because Mr Coombes was well practised and had a splendid aim. He was able, so it seemed, to land the second one almost across the narrow line where the first one had struck. It is bad enough when the cane lands on fresh skin, but when it comes down on bruised and wounded flesh, the agony is unbelievable.

The third one seemed even worse than the second. Whether or not the wily Mr Coombes had chalked the cane beforehand and had thus made an aiming mark on my grey flannel shorts after the first stroke, I do not know. I am inclined to doubt it because he must have known that this was a practice much frowned upon by Headmasters in general in those days. It was not only regarded as unsporting, it was also an admission that you were not an expert at the job.

By the time the fourth stroke was delivered, my entire backside seemed to be going up in flames.

Far away in the distance, I heard Mr Coombes's voice saying, 'Now get out.'

As I limped across the study clutching my buttocks hard with both hands, a cackling sound came from the armchair over in the corner, and then I heard the vinegary voice of Mrs Pratchett saying, 'I am very much obliged to you, 'Eadmaster, very much obliged. I don't think we is goin' to see any more stinkin' mice in my Gobstoppers from now on.'

When I returned to the classroom my eyes were wet with tears and everybody stared at me. My bottom hurt when I sat down at my desk.

That evening after supper my three sisters had their baths before me. Then it was my turn, but as I was about to step into the bathtub, I heard a horrified gasp from my mother behind me.

'What's this?' she gasped. 'What's happened to you?' She was staring at my bottom. I myself had not inspected it up to then, but when I twisted my head around and took a look at one of my buttocks, I saw the scarlet stripes and the deep blue bruising in between.

'Who did this?' my mother cried. 'Tell me at once!'

In the end I had to tell her the whole story, while my three sisters (aged nine, six and four) stood around in their nighties listening goggle-eyed. My mother heard me out in silence. She asked no questions. She just let me talk, and when I had finished, she said to our nurse, 'You get them into bed, Nanny. I'm going out.'

If I had had the slightest idea of what she was going to do next, I would have tried to stop her, but I hadn't. She went straight downstairs and put on her hat. Then she marched out of the house, down the drive and on to the road. I saw her through my bedroom window as she went out of the gates and turned left, and I remember calling out to her to come back, come back, come back. But she took no notice of me. She was walking very quickly, with her head held high and her body erect, and by the look of things I figured that Mr Coombes was in for a hard time.

About an hour later, my mother returned and came upstairs to kiss us all goodnight.

'I wish you hadn't done that,' I said to her. 'It makes me look silly.'

'They don't beat small children like that where I come from,' she said. 'I won't allow it.'

'What did Mr Coombes say to you, Mama?'

'He told me that I was a foreigner and I didn't understand how British schools were run,' she said.

'Did he get ratty with you?'

'Very ratty,' she said. 'He told me that if I didn't like his methods I could take you away.'

'What did you say?'

'I said I would, as soon as the school year is finished. I shall find you an *English* school this time,' she said. 'Your father was right. English schools are the best in the world.'

'Does that mean it'll be a boarding school?' I asked.

'It'll have to be,' she said. 'I am not quite ready to move the whole family to England yet.'

So I stayed on at Llandaff Cathedral School until the end of the summer term.

Going to Norway

The summer holidays! Those magic words! The mere mention of them used to send shivers of joy rippling over my skin.

All my summer holidays, from when I was four years old to when I was seventeen (1920–1932), were totally idyllic. This, I am certain, was because we always went to the same idyllic place and that place was Norway.

Except for my ancient half-sister and my not-quite-so-ancient half-brother, the rest of us were all pure Norwegian by blood. We all spoke Norwegian and all our relations lived over there. So in a way, going to Norway every summer was like going home.

Even the journey was an event. Do not forget that there were no commercial aeroplanes in those times, so it took us four whole days to complete the trip out and another four days to get home again.

We were always an enormous party. There were my three sisters and my ancient half-sister (that's four), and my half-brother and me (that's six), and my mother (that's seven), and Nanny (that's eight), and in addition to these, there were never less than two others who were some sort of anonymous ancient friends of the ancient half-sister (that's ten altogether).

Looking back on it now, I don't know how my mother did it. There were all those train bookings and boat bookings and hotel bookings to be made in advance by letter. She had to make sure that we had enough shorts and shirts and sweaters and gymshoes and bathing costumes (you couldn't even buy a shoelace on the island we were going to), and the packing must have been a nightmare. Six huge trunks were carefully packed, as well as countless suitcases, and when the great departure day arrived, the ten of us, together with our mountains of luggage, would set out on the first and easiest step of the journey, the train to London.

When we arrived in London, we tumbled into three taxis and went clattering across the great city to King's Cross, where we got on to the train for Newcastle, nearly three hundred miles to the north. The trip to Newcastle took about five hours, and when we arrived there, we needed three more taxis to take us from the station to the docks, where our boat would be waiting. The next stop after that would be Oslo, the capital of Norway.

When I was young, the capital of Norway was not called Oslo. It was called Christiania. But somewhere along the line, the Norwegians decided to do away with that pretty name and call it Oslo instead. As children, we always knew it as Christiania, but if I call it that here we shall only get confused, so I had better stick to Oslo all the way through.

The sea journey from Newcastle to Oslo took two days and a night, and if it was rough, as it often was, all of us got seasick except our dauntless mother. We used to lie in deck-chairs on the promenade deck, within easy reach of the rails, embalmed in rugs, our faces slatc-grey and our stomachs churning, refusing the hot soup and ship's biscuits the kindly steward kept offering us. And as for poor Nanny, she began to feel sick the moment she set foot on deck. 'I hate these things!' she used to say. 'I'm sure we'll never get there! Which lifeboat do we go to when it starts to sink?' Then she would retire to her cabin, where she stayed groaning and trembling until the ship was firmly tied up at the quayside in Oslo harbour the next day.

We always stopped off for one night in Oslo so that we could have a grand annual family reunion with Bestemama and Bestepapa, our mother's parents, and with her two maiden sisters (our aunts) who lived in the same house.

Bestemama and Bestepapa (and Astri)

When we got off the boat, we all went in a cavalcade of taxis straight to the Grand Hotel, where we would sleep one night, to drop off our luggage. Then, keeping the same taxis, we drove on to the grandparents' house, where an emotional welcome awaited us. All of us were embraced and kissed many times and tears flowed down wrinkled old cheeks and suddenly that quiet gloomy house came alive with many children's voices.

Ever since I first saw her, Bestemama was terrifically ancient. She was a white-haired wrinkly-faced old bird who seemed always to be sitting in her rocking-chair, rocking away and smiling benignly at this vast influx of grandchildren who barged in from miles away to take over her house for a few hours every year.

Bestepapa was the quiet one. He was a small dignified scholar with a white goatee beard, and as far as I could gather, he was an astrologer, a meteorologist and a speaker of ancient Greek. Like Bestemama, he sat most of the time quietly in a chair, saying very little and totally overwhelmed, I imagine, by the raucous rabble who were destroying his neat and polished home. The two things I remember most about

Bestepapa were that he wore black boots and that he smoked an extraordinary pipe. The bowl of his pipe was made of meerschaum clay, and it had a flexible stem about three feet long so that the bowl rested on his lap.

All the grown-ups including Nanny, and all the children, even when the youngest was only a year old, sat down around the big oval dining-room table on the afternoon of our arrival, for the great annual celebration feast with the grandparents, and the food we received never varied. This was a Norwegian household, and for the Norwegians the best food in the world is fish. And when they say fish, they don't mean the sort of thing you and I get from the fishmonger. They mean *fresh fish*, fish that has been caught no more than twenty-four hours before and has never been frozen or chilled on a block of ice. I agree with them that the proper way to prepare fish like this is to poach it, and that is what they do with the finest specimens. And Norwegians, by the way, always eat the skin of the boiled fish, which they say has the best taste of all.

So naturally this great celebration feast started with fish. A massive fish, a flounder as big as a tea-tray and as thick as your arm was brought to the table. It had nearly black skin on top which was covered with brilliant orange spots, and it had, of course, been perfectly poached. Large white hunks of this fish were carved out and put on to our plates, and with it we had hollandaise sauce and boiled new potatoes. Nothing else. And by gosh, it was delicious.

As soon as the remains of the fish had been cleared away, a tremendous craggy mountain of home-made ice-cream would be carried in. Apart from being the creamiest ice-cream in the world, the flavour was unforgettable. There were thousands of little chips of crisp burnt toffee mixed into it (the Norwegians call it *krokan*), and as a result it didn't simply melt in your mouth like ordinary ice-cream. You chewed it and it went *crunch* and the taste was something you dreamed about for days afterwards.

This great feast would be interrupted by a small speech of welcome from my grandfather, and the grown-ups would raise their long-stemmed wine glasses and say 'skaal' many times throughout the meal.

When the guzzling was over, those who were considered old enough were given small glasses of home-made liqueur, a colourless but fiery drink that smelled of mulberries. The glasses were raised again and again, and the 'skaaling' seemed to go on for ever. In Norway, you may select any individual around the table and skaal him or her in a small private ceremony. You first lift your glass high and call out the name. 'Bestemama!' you say. 'Skaal, Bestemama!' She will then lift her own glass and hold it up high. At the same time your own eyes meet hers, and you *must* keep looking deep into her eyes as you sip your drink. After you have both done this, you raise your glasses high up again in a sort of silent final salute, and only then does each person look away and set down his glass. It is a serious and solemn ceremony, and as a rule on formal occasions everyone skaals everyone else round the table once. If there are, for example, ten people present and you are one of them, you will skaal your nine companions once each individually, and you yourself will also receive nine separate skaals at different times during the meal – eighteen in all. That's how they work it in polite society over there, at least they used to in the old days, and quite a business it was. By the time I was ten, I would be permitted to take part in these ceremonies, and I always finished up as tipsy as a lord.

The Magic Island

The next morning, everyone got up early
and eager to continue the journey. There was
another full day's travelling to be done before
we reached our final destination, most of it by
boat. So after a rapid breakfast, our cavalcade
left the Grand Hotel in three more taxis and
headed for Oslo docks. There we went on
board a small coastal steamer, and Nanny was
heard to say, 'I'm sure it leaks! We shall all
be food for the fishes before the day is out!'
Then she would disappear below for the rest
of the trip.

We loved this part of the journey. The splendid little vessel with its single tall funnel would move out into the calm waters of the fjord and proceed at a leisurely pace along the coast, stopping every hour or so at a small wooden jetty where a group of villagers and summer people would be waiting to welcome friends or to collect parcels and mail. Unless you have sailed down the Oslofjord like this yourself on a tranquil summer's day, you cannot imagine what it is like. It is impossible to describe the sensation of absolute peace and beauty that surrounds you. The boat weaves in and out between countless tiny islands, some with small brightly painted wooden houses on them, but many with not a house or a tree on the bare rocks. These granite rocks are so smooth that you can lie and sun yourself on them in your bathing-costume without putting a towel underneath. We would see long-legged girls and tall boys basking on the rocks of the islands. There are no sandy beaches on the fjord. The rocks go straight down to the water's edge and the water is immediately deep. As a result, Norwegian children all learn to swim when they are very young because if you can't swim it is difficult to find a place to bathe.

Sometimes when our little vessel slipped between two small islands, the channel was so narrow we could almost touch the rocks on either side. We would pass row-boats and canoes with flaxen-haired children in them, their skins browned by the sun, and we would wave to them and watch their tiny boats rocking violently in the swell that our larger ship left behind.

Late in the afternoon, we would come finally to the end of the journey, the island of Tjöme. This was where our mother always took us. Heaven knows how she found it, but to us it was the greatest place on earth. About two hundred yards from the jetty, along a narrow dusty road, stood a simple wooden hotel painted white. It was run by an elderly couple whose faces I still remember vividly, and every year they welcomed us like old friends. Everything about the hotel was extremely primitive, except the dining-room. The walls, the ceiling and the floor of our bedrooms were made of plain unvarnished pine planks. There was a washbasin and a jug of cold water in each of them. The lavatories were in a rickety wooden outhouse at the back of the hotel and each cubicle contained nothing more than a round hole cut in a piece of wood. You sat on the hole and what you did there dropped into a pit ten feet below. If you looked down the hole, you would often see rats scurrying about in the gloom. All this we took for granted.

Breakfast was the best meal of the day in our hotel, and it was all laid out on a huge table in the middle of the dining-room from which you helped yourself. There were maybe fifty different dishes to choose from on that table. There were large jugs of milk, which all Norwegian children drink at every meal. There were plates of cold beef, veal, ham and pork. There was cold boiled mackerel submerged in aspic. There were spiced and pickled herring fillets, sardines, smoked eels and cod's roe. There was a large bowl piled high with hot boiled eggs. There were cold omelettes with chopped ham in them, and cold chicken and hot coffee for the grown-ups, and hot crisp rolls baked in the hotel kitchen, which we ate with butter and cranberry jam. There were stewed apricots and five or six different cheeses including of course the ever-present gjetost, that tall brown, rather sweet Norwegian goat's cheese which you find on just about every table in the land.

After breakfast, we collected our bathing things and the whole party, all ten of us, would pile into our boat.

Everyone has some sort of boat in Norway. Nobody sits around in front of the hotel. Nor does anyone sit on the beach because there aren't any beaches to sit on. In the early days, we had only a row-boat, but a very fine one it was. It carried all of us easily, with places for two rowers. My mother took one pair of

oars and my fairly ancient half-brother took
the other, and off we would go.

me, Alfhild, Else Norway 1924

My mother and the half-brother (he was
somewhere around eighteen then) were expert
rowers. They kept in perfect time and the
oars went *click-click, click-click* in their wooden
rowlocks, and the rowers never paused once
during the long forty-minute journey. The
rest of us sat in the boat trailing our fingers
in the clear water and looking for jellyfish. We
skimmed across the sound and went whizzing
through narrow channels with rocky islands on
either side, heading as always for a very secret

tiny patch of sand on a distant island that only we knew about. In the early days we needed a place like this where we could paddle and play about because my youngest sister was only one, the next sister was three and I was four. The rocks and the deep water were no good to us.

Every day, for several summers, that tiny secret sand-patch on that tiny secret island was our regular destination. We would stay there for three or four hours, messing about in the water and in the rockpools and getting extra-ordinarily sunburnt.

In later years, when we were all a little older and could swim, the daily routine became different. By then, my mother had acquired a motor-boat, a small and not very seaworthy white wooden vessel which sat far too low in the water and was powered by an unreliable one-cylinder engine. The fairly ancient half-brother was the only one who could make the engine go at all. It was extremely difficult to start, and he always had to unscrew the sparking-plug and pour petrol into the cylinder. Then he swung a flywheel round and round, and with a bit of luck, after a lot of coughing and spluttering, the thing would finally get going.

When we first acquired the motor-boat, my

youngest sister was four and I was seven, and by then all of us had learnt to swim. The exciting new boat made it possible for us to go much farther afield, and every day we would travel far out into the fjord, hunting for a different island. There were hundreds of them to choose from. Some were very small, no more than thirty yards long. Others were quite large, maybe half a mile in length. It was wonderful to have such a choice of places, and it was terrific fun to explore each island before we went swimming off the rocks. There were the wooden skeletons of shipwrecked boats on those islands, and big white bones (were they human bones?), and wild raspberries, and mussels clinging to the rocks, and some of the islands had shaggy long-haired goats on them, and even sheep.

Now and again, when we were out in the open water beyond the chain of islands, the sea became very rough, and that was when my mother enjoyed herself most. Nobody, not even the tiny children, bothered with lifebelts in those days. We would cling to the sides of our funny little white motor-boat, driving through mountainous white-capped waves and getting drenched to the skin, while my mother calmly handled the tiller. There were times, I promise you, when the waves were so high that as we slid down into a trough the whole world disappeared from sight. Then up and up the little boat would climb, standing almost vertically on its tail, until we reached the crest of the next wave, and then it was like being on top of a foaming mountain. It requires great skill to handle a small boat in seas like these. The thing can easily capsize or be swamped if the bows do not meet the great combing breakers at just the right angle. But my mother knew exactly how to do it, and we were never afraid. We loved every minute of it, all of us except for our long-suffering Nanny, who would bury her face in her hands and call aloud upon the Lord to save her soul.

In the early evenings we nearly always went

out fishing. We collected mussels from the rocks for bait, then we got into either the row-boat or the motor-boat and pushed off to drop anchor later in some likely spot. The water was very deep and often we had to let out two hundred feet of line before we touched bottom. We would sit silent and tense, waiting for a bite, and it always amazed me how even a little nibble at the end of that long line would be transmitted to one's fingers. 'A bite!' someone would shout, jerking the line. 'I've got him! It's a big one! It's a whopper!' And then came the thrill of hauling in the line hand over hand and peering over the side into the clear water to see how big the fish really was as he neared the surface. Cod, whiting, haddock and mackerel, we caught them all and bore them back triumphantly to the hotel kitchen where the cheery fat woman who did the cooking promised to get them ready for our supper.

I tell you, my friends, those were the days.

A Visit to the Doctor

I have only one unpleasant memory of the summer holidays in Norway. We were in the grandparents' house in Oslo and my mother said to me, 'We are going to the doctor this afternoon. He wants to look at your nose and mouth.'

I think I was eight at the time. 'What's wrong with my nose and mouth?' I asked.

'Nothing much,' my mother said. 'But I think you've got adenoids.'

'What are *they*?' I asked her.

'Don't worry about it,' she said. 'It's nothing.'

I held my mother's hand as we walked to the doctor's house. It took us about half an hour. There was a kind of dentist's chair in the surgery and I was lifted into it. The doctor had a round mirror strapped to his forehead and he peered up my nose and into my mouth. He then took my mother aside and they held a whispered conversation. I saw my mother looking rather grim, but she nodded.

The doctor now put some water to boil in an aluminium mug over a gas flame, and into the boiling water he placed a long thin shiny steel instrument. I sat there watching the steam coming off the boiling water. I was not in the least apprehensive. I was too young to realize that something out of the ordinary was going to happen.

Then a nurse dressed in white came in. She was carrying a red rubber apron and a curved white enamel bowl. She put the apron over the front of my body and tied it around my neck. It was far too big. Then she held the enamel bowl under my chin. The curve of the bowl fitted perfectly against the curve of my chest.

The doctor was bending over me. In his hand he held that long shiny steel instrument. He held it right in front of my face, and to this day I can still describe it perfectly. It was about the thickness and length of a pencil, and like most pencils it had a lot of sides to it. Towards the end, the metal became much thinner, and at the very end of the thin bit of metal there was a tiny blade set at an angle. The blade wasn't more than a centimetre long, very small, very sharp and very shiny.

'Open your mouth,' the doctor said, speaking Norwegian.

I refused. I thought he was going to do something to my teeth, and everything anyone had ever done to my teeth had been painful.

'It won't take two seconds,' the doctor said. He spoke gently, and I was seduced by his voice. Like an ass, I opened my mouth.

The tiny blade flashed in the bright light and disappeared into my mouth. It went high up into the roof of my mouth, and the hand that held the blade gave four or five very quick little twists and the next moment, out of my mouth into the basin came tumbling a whole mass of flesh and blood.

I was too shocked and outraged to do anything but yelp. I was horrified by the huge red lumps that had fallen out of my mouth into the white basin and my first thought was that the doctor had cut out the whole of the middle of my head.

'Those were your adenoids,' I heard the doctor saying.

I sat there gasping. The roof of my mouth

seemed to be on fire. I grabbed my mother's hand and held on to it tight. I couldn't believe that anyone would do this to me.

'Stay where you are,' the doctor said. 'You'll be all right in a minute.'

Blood was still coming out of my mouth and dripping into the basin the nurse was holding. 'Spit it all out,' she said, 'there's a good boy.'

'You'll be able to breathe much better through your nose after this,' the doctor said.

The nurse wiped my lips and washed my face with a wet flannel. Then they lifted me out of the chair and stood me on my feet. I felt a bit groggy.

'We'll get you home,' my mother said, taking my hand. Down the stairs we went and on to the street. We started walking. I said *walking*. No trolley-car or taxi. We walked the full half-hour journey back to my grandparents' house, and when we arrived at last, I can remember as clearly as anything my grandmother saying, 'Let him sit down in that chair and rest for a while. After all, he's had an operation.'

Someone placed a chair for me beside my grandmother's armchair, and I sat down. My grandmother reached over and covered one of my hands in both of hers. 'That won't be the last time you'll go to a doctor in your life,' she said. 'And with a bit of luck, they won't do you too much harm.'

That was in 1924, and taking out a child's adenoids, and often the tonsils as well, without any anaesthetic was common practice in those days. I wonder, though, what you would think if some doctor did that to you today.

St Peter's, 1925–9

(age 9–13)

St. Peters uniform

Jack Hobbs
Cumberland Lodge Llandaff

Duckworth Butterflies my house
St. Peters
me in front row

Asta Else Alfhild me
Cardiff 1927

First Day

In September 1925, when I was just nine, I set out on the first great adventure of my life – boarding-school. My mother had chosen for me a Prep School in a part of England which was as near as it could possibly be to our home in South Wales, and it was called St Peter's. The full postal address was St Peter's School, Weston-super-Mare, Somerset.

Weston-super-Mare is a slightly seedy seaside resort with a vast sandy beach, a tremendous long pier, an esplanade running along the sea-front, a clutter of hotels and boarding-houses, and about ten thousand little shops selling buckets and spades and sticks of rock and ice-creams. It lies almost directly across the Bristol Channel from Cardiff, and on a clear day you can stand on the esplanade at Weston and look across the fifteen or so miles of water and see the coast of Wales lying pale and milky on the horizon.

In those days the easiest way to travel from Cardiff to Weston-super-Mare was by boat. Those boats were beautiful. They were paddle-steamers, with gigantic swishing paddle-wheels on their flanks, and the wheels made the most terrific noise as they sloshed and churned through the water.

On the first day of my first term I set out by taxi in the afternoon with my mother to catch the paddle steamer from Cardiff Docks to Weston-super-Mare. Every piece of clothing I wore was brand new and had my name on it. I wore black shoes, grey woollen stockings with blue turnovers, grey flannel shorts, a grey shirt, a red tie, a grey flannel blazer with the blue school crest on the breast pocket and a grey school cap with the same crest just above the peak. Into the taxi that was taking us to the docks went my brand new trunk and my brand new tuck-box, and both had R. DAHL painted on them in black.

A tuck-box is a small pinewood trunk which is very strongly made, and no boy has ever gone as a boarder to any English Prep School without one. It is his own secret store-house,

as secret as a lady's handbag, and there is an
unwritten law that no other boy, no teacher,
not even the Headmaster himself has the right
to pry into the contents of your tuck-box.
The owner has the key in his pocket and that
is where it stays. At St Peter's, the tuck-boxes
were ranged shoulder to shoulder all around
the four walls of the changing-room and your
own tuck-box stood directly below the peg on
which you hung your games clothes. A tuck-
box, as the name implies, is a box in which
you store your tuck. At Prep School in those
days, a parcel of tuck was sent once a week
by anxious mothers to their ravenous little
sons, and an average tuck-box would probably
contain, at almost any time, half a home-made
currant cake, a packet of squashed-fly biscuits,

a couple of oranges, an apple, a banana, a pot of strawberry jam or Marmite, a bar of chocolate, a bag of Liquorice Allsorts and a tin of Bassett's lemonade powder. An English school in those days was purely a money-making business owned and operated by the Headmaster. It suited him, therefore, to give the boys as little food as possible himself and to encourage the parents in various cunning ways to feed their offspring by parcel-post from home.

'By all means, my dear Mrs Dahl, *do* send your boy some little treats now and again,' he would say. 'Perhaps a few oranges and apples once a week' – fruit was very expensive – 'and a nice currant cake, a *large* currant cake perhaps because small boys have large appetites do they not, ha-ha-ha ...Yes, yes, as *often* as you like. More than once a week if you wish ... *Of course* he'll be getting plenty of good food here, the best there is, but it never tastes *quite* the same as home cooking, does it? I'm sure you wouldn't want him to be the only one who doesn't get a lovely parcel from home every week.'

As well as tuck, a tuck-box would also contain all manner of treasures such as a magnet, a pocket-knife, a compass, a ball of string, a clockwork racing-car, half-a-dozen lead soldiers,

a box of conjuring-tricks, some tiddly-winks, a
Mexican jumping bean, a catapult, some foreign
stamps, a couple of stink-bombs, and I remember
one boy called Arkle who drilled an airhole in
the lid of his tuck-box and kept a pet frog in
there which he fed on slugs.

So off we set, my mother and I and my trunk
and my tuck-box, and we boarded the paddle-
steamer and went swooshing across the Bristol
Channel in a shower of spray. I liked that part
of it, but I began to grow apprehensive as I
disembarked on to the pier at Weston-super-
Mare and watched my trunk and tuck-box
being loaded into an English taxi which would
drive us to St Peter's. I had absolutely no idea

what was in store for me. I had never spent a single night away from our large family before.

St Peter's was on a hill above the town. It was a long three-storeyed stone building that looked rather like a private lunatic asylum, and in front of it lay the playing-fields with their three football pitches. One-third of the building was reserved for the Headmaster and his family. The rest of it housed the boys, about one hundred and fifty of them altogether, if I remember rightly.

the Loony Bin!

As we got out of the taxi, I saw the whole driveway abustle with small boys and their parents and their trunks and their tuck-boxes, and a man I took to be the Headmaster was swimming around among them shaking everybody by the hand.

I have already told you that *all* Headmasters are giants, and this one was no exception. He advanced upon my mother and shook her by the hand, then he shook me by the hand and as he did so he gave me the kind of flashing grin a shark might give to a small fish just before he gobbles it up. One of his front teeth, I noticed, was edged all the way round with gold, and his hair was slicked down with so much hair-cream that it glistened like butter.

'Right,' he said to me. 'Off you go and report to the Matron.' And to my mother he said briskly, 'Goodbye, Mrs Dahl. I shouldn't linger if I were you. We'll look after him.'

My mother got the message. She kissed me on the cheek and said goodbye and climbed right back into the taxi.

The Headmaster moved away to another group and I was left standing there beside my brand new trunk and my brand new tuck-box. I began to cry.

Writing Home

At St Peter's, Sunday morning was letter-writing time. At nine o'clock the whole school had to go to their desks and spend one hour writing a letter home to their parents. At ten-fifteen we put on our caps and coats and formed up outside the school in a long crocodile and marched a couple of miles down into Weston-super-Mare for church, and we didn't get back until lunchtime. Church going never became a habit with me. Letter-writing did.

Here is the very first letter I wrote home from St Peter's.

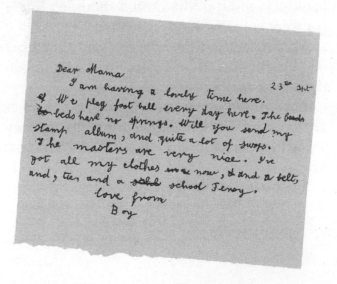

Dear Mama
    I am having a lovely time here.
We play foot ball every day here. The beds
have no springs. Will you send my
Stamp album, and quite a lot of swops.
The masters are very nice. I've
got all my clothes now, and a belt,
and, ties and a school Jersy.
        love from
        Boy

From that very first Sunday at St Peter's until the day my mother died thirty-two years later, I wrote to her once a week, sometimes more often, whenever I was away from home. I wrote to her every week from St Peter's (I had to), and every week from my next school, Repton, and every week from Dar es Salaam in East Africa, where I went on my first job after leaving school, and then every week during the war from Kenya and Iraq and Egypt when I was flying with the R.A.F.

... —o Major Cottam is going to recite something caled "as you like it" To night. Plese could you send me some conkers as quick as you can, but dont dont send To meny, the just send them in a Tin and wrapit up in paper

My mother, for her part, kept every one of these letters, binding them carefully in neat bundles with green tape, but this was her own secret. She never told me she was doing it. In 1957, when she knew she was dying, I was in hospital in Oxford having a serious operation on my spine and I was unable to write to her.

So she had a telephone specially installed beside her bed in order that she might have one last conversation with me. She didn't tell me she was dying nor did anyone else for that matter because I was in a fairly serious condition myself at the time. She simply asked me how I was and hoped I would get better soon and sent me her love. I had no idea that she would die the next day, but *she* knew all right and she wanted to reach out and speak to me for the last time.

When I recovered and went home, I was given this vast collection of my letters, all so neatly bound with green tape, more than six hundred of them altogether, dating from 1925 to 1945, each one in its original envelope with the old stamps still on them. I am awfully lucky to have something like this to refer to in my old age.

Letter-writing was a serious business at St Peter's. It was as much a lesson in spelling and punctuation as anything else because the Headmaster would patrol the classrooms all through the session, peering over our shoulders to read what we were writing and to point out our mistakes. But that, I am quite sure, was not the main reason for his interest. He was there to make sure that we said nothing horrid about his school.

This is my Christmas wish list, as far as I can see.
A mashie-niblick, (which I have to close).
A decent book.
I cant think of any thing else: If you send me a catalogue I might be able to tell you.

There was no way, therefore, that we could ever complain to our parents about anything during term-time. If we thought the food was lousy or if we hated a certain master or if we had been thrashed for something we did not do, we never dared to say so in our letters. In fact, we often went the other way. In order to please that dangerous Headmaster who was leaning over our shoulders and reading what we had written, we would say splendid things about the school and go on about how lovely the masters were.

> , *a man called Mr Nichell gave us a fine lecture last knight on birds, he told us how owls owls eat mice they eat the hole mouse skin and all, and then all the skin and bones goes into a sort of little paw parsel in side him and he puts it on the ground, and those are caled pelets, and he showed us some pictures of some witch he has found, and of fotes of other Birds.*

Mind you, the Headmaster was a clever fellow. He did not want our parents to think that those letters of ours were censored in this way, and therefore he never allowed us to correct a spelling mistake in the letter itself. If, for example, I had written . . . *last Tuesday knight we had a lecture* . . . , he would say:

'Don't you know how to spell night?'

'Y-yes, sir, k–n–i–g–h–t.'

'That's the other kind of knight, you idiot!'

'Which kind, sir? I . . . I don't understand.'

'The one in shining armour! The man on horseback! How do you spell Tuesday night?'

'I ... I ... I'm not quite sure, sir.'

'It's n–i–g–h–t, boy, n–i–g–h–t. Stay in and write it out for me fifty times this afternoon. No, no! Don't change it in the letter! You don't want to make it any messier than it is! It must go as you wrote it!'

Thus, the unsuspecting parents received in this subtle way the impression that your letter had never been seen or censored or corrected by anyone.

Jan. 27th 1928.

St Peter's
Weston-super-mare.

Dear Mama

Thank you very much for the cake etc. I got the book the day before yesterday; quite a nice edition. How are the chicks? hope they'll all live. By the way, you said she would'nt get any.

The Matron

At St Peter's the ground floor was all classrooms. The first floor was all dormitories. On the dormitory floor the Matron ruled supreme. This was her territory. Hers was the only voice of authority up here, and even the eleven- and twelve-year-old boys were terrified of this female ogre, for she ruled with a rod of steel.

The Matron was a large fair-haired woman with a bosom. Her age was probably no more than twenty-eight but it made no difference whether she was twenty-eight or sixty-eight because to us a grown-up was a grown-up and all grown-ups were dangerous creatures at this school.

Once you had climbed to the top of the stairs and set foot on the dormitory floor, you were in Matron's power, and the source of this power was the unseen but frightening figure of the Headmaster lurking down in the depths of his study below. At any time she liked, the Matron could send you down in your pyjamas and dressing-gown to report to this merciless giant, and whenever this happened you got caned on the spot. The Matron knew this and she relished the whole business.

She could move along that corridor like lightning, and when you least expected it, her head and her bosom would come popping through the dormitory doorway. 'Who threw that sponge?' the dreaded voice would call out. 'It was *you*, Perkins, was it not? Don't lie to me, Perkins! Don't argue with me! I know perfectly well it was you! Now you can put your dressing-gown on and go downstairs and report to the Headmaster this instant!'

In slow motion and with immense reluctance, little Perkins, aged eight and a half, would get into his dressing-gown and slippers and disappear down the long corridor that led to the back stairs and the Headmaster's private quarters. And the Matron, as we all knew, would follow after him and stand at the top of the stairs listening with a funny look on her face for the *crack . . . crack . . . crack* of the cane that would soon be coming up from below. To me that noise always sounded as though the Headmaster was firing a pistol at the ceiling of his study.

Looking back on it now, there seems little doubt that the Matron disliked small boys very much indeed. She never smiled at us or said anything nice, and when for example the lint stuck to the cut on your kneecap, you were not allowed to take it off yourself bit by bit so that it didn't hurt. She would always whip it off with a flourish, muttering, 'Don't be such a ridiculous little baby!'

'We've got a new matron. Last term, one night in the washing room, having inspected a boy called Ford she kissed him and ...

On one occasion during my first term, I went down to the Matron's room to have some iodine put on a grazed knee and I didn't know you had to knock before you entered. I opened the door and walked right in, and there she was in the centre of the Sick Room floor locked in some kind of an embrace with the Latin master, Mr Victor Corrado. They flew apart as I entered and both their faces went suddenly crimson.

'How *dare* you come in without knocking!' the Matron shouted. 'Here I am trying to get something out of Mr Corrado's eye and in you burst and disturb the whole delicate operation!'

'I'm very sorry, Matron.'

'Go away and come back in five minutes!' she cried, and I shot out of the room like a bullet.

After 'lights out' the Matron would prowl the corridor like a panther trying to catch the sound of a whisper behind a dormitory door, and we soon learnt that her powers of hearing were so phenomenal that it was safer to keep quiet.

Once, after lights out, a brave boy called Wragg tiptoed out of our dormitory and sprink-led castor sugar all over the linoleum floor of the corridor. When Wragg returned and told us that the corridor had been successfully sugared from one end to the other, I began shivering with excitement. I lay there in the dark in my bed waiting and waiting for the Matron to go on the prowl. Nothing happened. Perhaps, I told myself, she is in her room taking another speck of dust out of Mr Victor Corrado's eye.

Suddenly, from far down the corridor came a resounding *crunch*! *Crunch crunch crunch* went the footsteps. It sounded as though a giant was walking on loose gravel.

Then we heard the high-pitched furious voice of the Matron in the distance. 'Who did this?' she was shrieking. 'How *dare* you do this!' She went crunching along the corridor flinging open all the dormitory doors and switching on all the lights. The intensity of her fury was frightening. 'Come along!' she cried out, marching with crunching steps up and down the corridor. 'Own up! I want the name of the filthy little boy who put down the sugar! Own up immediately! Step forward! Confess!'

'Don't own up,' we whispered to Wragg. 'We won't give you away!'

Wragg kept quiet. I didn't blame him for that. Had he owned up, it was certain his fate would have been a terrible and a bloody one.

Soon the Headmaster was summoned from below. The Matron, with steam coming out of her nostrils, cried out to him for help and now the whole school was herded into the long corridor, where we stood freezing in our pyjamas and bare feet while the culprit or culprits were ordered to step forward.

Nobody stepped forward.

I could see that the Headmaster was getting very angry indeed. His evening had been interrupted. Red splotches were appearing all over his face and flecks of spit were shooting out of his mouth as he talked.

'Very well!' he thundered. 'Every one of you will go at once and get the key to his tuck-box! Hand the keys to Matron, who will keep them for the rest of the term! And all parcels coming from home will be confiscated from now on! I will not tolerate this kind of behaviour!'

We handed in our keys and throughout the remaining six weeks of the term we went very hungry. But all through those six weeks, Arkle continued to feed his frog with slugs through the hole in the lid of his tuck-box. Using an old teapot, he also poured water in through the hole every day to keep the creature moist and happy. I admired Arkle very much for looking after his frog so well. Although he himself was famished, he refused to let his frog go hungry. Ever since then I have tried to be kind to small animals.

Each dormitory had about twenty beds in it. These were smallish narrow beds ranged along the walls on either side. Down the centre of the dormitory stood the basins where you washed your hands and face and did your teeth, always with cold water which stood in large jugs on the floor. Once you had entered the dormitory, you were not allowed to leave it unless you were reporting to the Matron's room with some sickness or injury. Under each bed there was a white chamber-pot, and before getting into bed you were expected to kneel on the floor and empty your bladder into it. All around the dormitory, just before 'lights out', was heard the *tinkle-tinkle* of little boys peeing into their pots. Once you had done this and got into your bed, you were not allowed to get out of it again until next morning. There was, I believe, a lavatory somewhere along the corridor, but only an attack of acute diarrhoea would be accepted as an excuse for visiting it. A journey to the upstairs lavatory automatically classed you as a diarrhoea victim, and a dose of thick white liquid would immediately be forced down your throat by the Matron. This made you constipated for a week.

Thanks for your letter. There are exactly 23 boys with the measles and all the other schools (boys) in here have got it. Hope Louis hasn't had anything else wrong

The first miserable homesick night at St Peter's, when I curled up in bed and the lights were put out, I could think of nothing but our house at home and my mother and my sisters. Where were they? I asked myself. In which direction from where I was lying was Llandaff?

I began to work it out and it wasn't difficult to do this because I had the Bristol Channel to help me. If I looked out of the dormitory window I could see the Channel itself, and the big city of Cardiff with Llandaff alongside it lay almost directly across the water but slightly to the north. Therefore, if I turned towards the window I would be facing home. I wriggled round in my bed and faced my home and my family.

From then on, during all the time I was at St Peter's, I never went to sleep with my back to my family. Different beds in different dormitories required the working out of new directions, but the Bristol Channel was always my guide and I was always able to draw an imaginary line from my bed to our house over in Wales. Never once did I go to sleep looking away from my family. It was a great comfort to do this.

Do you know that a chap called Ford has got double Pneumonia on top of measles!!!!!! we've all got to be like mice going up to bed.

There was a boy in our dormitory during my first term called Tweedie, who one night started snoring soon after he had gone to sleep.

'Who's that talking?' cried the Matron, bursting in. My own bed was close to the door, and I remember looking up at her from my pillow and seeing her standing there silhouetted against the light from the corridor and thinking how truly frightening she looked. I think it was her enormous bosom that scared me most of all. My eyes were riveted to it, and to me it was like a battering-ram or the bows of an icebreaker or maybe a couple of high-explosive bombs.

'Own up!' she cried. 'Who was talking?'

We lay there in silence. Then Tweedie, who was lying fast asleep on his back with his mouth open, gave another snore.

The Matron stared at Tweedie. 'Snoring is a disgusting habit,' she said. 'Only the lower classes do it. We shall have to teach him a lesson.'

She didn't switch on the light, but she advanced into the room and picked up a cake of soap from the nearest basin. The bare electric bulb in the corridor illuminated the whole dormitory in a pale creamy glow.

None of us dared to sit up in bed, but all eyes were on the Matron now, watching to see what she was going to do next. She always had a pair of scissors hanging by a white tape from her waist, and with this she began shaving thin slivers of soap into the palm of one hand. Then she went over to where the wretched Tweedie lay and very carefully she dropped these little soap-flakes into his open mouth. She had a whole handful of them and I thought she was never going to stop.

What on earth was going to happen? I wondered. Would Tweedie choke? Would he strangle? Might his throat get blocked up completely? Was she going to kill him?

The Matron stepped back a couple of paces and folded her arms across, or rather underneath, her massive chest.

Nothing happened. Tweedie kept right on snoring.

Then suddenly he began to gurgle and white bubbles appeared around his lips. The bubbles grew and grew until in the end his whole face seemed to be smothered in a bubbly foaming white soapy froth. It was a horrific sight. Then all at once, Tweedie gave a great cough and a splutter and he sat up very fast and began clawing at his face with his hands. 'Oh!' he stuttered. 'Oh! Oh! Oh! Oh no! Wh-wh-what's happening? Wh-wh-what's on my face? Somebody help me!'

The Matron threw him a face flannel and said, 'Wipe it off, Tweedie. And don't ever let me hear you snoring again. Hasn't anyone ever taught you not to go to sleep on your back?'

With that she marched out of the dormitory and slammed the door.

very bad, he got better on Friday but has again got very ill. P.S. We have just been informed that poor little Ford died early this morning. Ford is still

Homesickness

I was homesick during the whole of my first term at St Peter's. Homesickness is a bit like seasickness. You don't know how awful it is till you get it, and when you do, it hits you right in the top of the stomach and you want to die. The only comfort is that both homesickness and seasickness are instantly curable. The first goes away the moment you walk out of the school grounds and the second is forgotten as soon as the ship enters port.

I was so devastatingly homesick during my first two weeks that I set about devising a stunt for getting myself sent back home, even if it were only for a few days. My idea was that I should all of a sudden develop an attack of acute appendicitis.

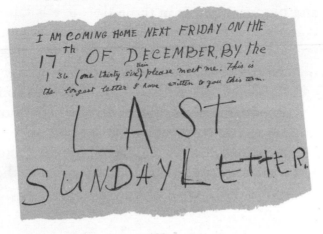

I AM COMING HOME NEXT FRIDAY ON THE 17Th OF DECEMBER, BY the 1 36 (one thirty six) *train* please meet me. This is the longest letter I have written to you this term.

LAST SUNDAY LETTER.

You will probably think it is silly that a nine-year-old boy should imagine he could get away with a trick like that, but I had sound reasons for trying it on. Only about a month before, my ancient half-sister, who was twelve years older than me, had actually *had* appendicitis, and for several days before her operation I was able to observe her behaviour at close quarters. I noticed that the thing she complained about most was a severe pain down in the lower right side of her tummy. As well as this, she kept being sick and refused to eat and ran a temperature.

You might, by the way, be interested to know that this sister had her appendix removed not in a fine hospital operating-room full of bright lights and gowned nurses but on our own nursery table at home by the local doctor and his anaesthetist. In those days it was fairly common practice for a doctor to arrive at your own house with a bag of instruments, then drape a sterile sheet over the most convenient table and get on with it. On this occasion, I can remember lurking in the corridor outside the nursery while the operation was going on. My other sisters were with me, and we stood there spellbound, listening to the soft medical murmurs coming from behind the locked door and picturing the patient with her stomach sliced open like a lump of beef. We could even smell the sickly fumes of ether filtering through the crack under the door.

The next day, we were allowed to inspect the appendix itself in a glass bottle. It was a longish black wormy-looking thing, and I said, 'Do *I* have one of those inside me, Nanny?'

'Everybody has one,' Nanny answered.

'What's it for?' I asked her.

'God works in his mysterious ways,' she said, which was her stock reply whenever she didn't know the answer.

'What makes it go bad?' I asked her.

'Toothbrush bristles,' she answered, this time with no hesitation at all.

'*Toothbrush* bristles?' I cried. 'How can *toothbrush* bristles make your appendix go bad?'

Nanny, who in my eyes was filled with more wisdom than Solomon, replied, 'Whenever a bristle comes out of your toothbrush and you swallow it, it sticks in your appendix and turns it rotten. In the war,' she went on, 'the German spies used to sneak boxloads of loose-bristled toothbrushes into our shops and millions of our soldiers got appendicitis.'

'Honestly, Nanny?' I cried. 'Is that honestly true?'

'I never lie to you, child,' she answered. 'So let that be a lesson to you never to use an old toothbrush.'

Thanks awfully for the tooth-paste and brush, and the choclate. I am now in training, and not allowed to eat anything except fruit (6...

For years after that, I used to get nervous whenever I found a toothbrush bristle on my tongue.

As I went upstairs and knocked on the brown door after breakfast, I didn't even feel frightened of the Matron.

'Come in!' boomed the voice.

I entered the room clutching my stomach on the right-hand side and staggering pathetically.

'What's the matter with you?' the Matron shouted, and the sheer force of her voice caused that massive bosom to quiver like a gigantic blancmange.

'It hurts, Matron,' I moaned. 'Oh, it hurts so much! Just here!'

'You've been over-eating!' she barked. 'What do you expect if you guzzle currant cake all day long!'

'I haven't eaten a thing for days,' I lied. 'I *couldn't* eat, Matron! I simply *couldn't*!'

'Get on the bed and lower your trousers,' she ordered.

I lay on the bed and she began prodding my tummy violently with her fingers. I was watching her carefully, and when she hit what I guessed was the appendix place, I let out a yelp that rattled the window-panes. 'Ow! Ow! Ow!' I cried out. 'Don't, Matron, don't!' Then I slipped in the clincher. 'I've been sick all morning,' I moaned, 'and now there's nothing left to be sick with, but I still feel sick!'

This was the right move. I saw her hesitate. 'Stay where you are,' she said and she walked quickly from the room. She may have been a foul and beastly woman, but she had had a nurse's training and she didn't want a ruptured appendix on her hands.

Within an hour, the doctor arrived and he

went through the same prodding and poking and I did my yelping at what I thought were the proper times. Then he put a thermometer in my mouth.

'Hmm,' he said. 'It reads normal. Let me feel your stomach once more.'

'Owch!' I screamed when he touched the vital spot.

The doctor went away with the Matron. The Matron returned half an hour later and said, 'The Headmaster has telephoned your mother and she's coming to fetch you this afternoon.'

I didn't answer her. I just lay there trying to look very ill, but my heart was singing out with all sorts of wonderful songs of praise and joy.

I was taken home across the Bristol Channel on the paddle-steamer and I felt so wonderful at being away from that dreaded school building that I very nearly forgot I was meant to be ill. That afternoon I had a session with Dr Dunbar at his surgery in Cathedral Road, Cardiff, and I tried the same tricks all over again. But Dr Dunbar was far wiser and more skilful than either the Matron or the school doctor. After he had prodded my stomach and I had done my yelping routine, he said to me, 'Now you can get dressed again and seat yourself on that chair.'

He himself sat down behind his desk and fixed me with a penetrating but not unkindly eye. 'You're faking, aren't you?' he said.

'How do you know?' I blurted out.

'Because your stomach is soft and perfectly normal,' he answered. 'If you had had any inflammation down there, the stomach would have been hard and rigid. It's quite easy to tell.'

I kept silent.

'I expect you're homesick,' he said.

I nodded miserably.

'Everyone is at first,' he said. 'You have to stick it out. And don't blame your mother for sending you away to boarding-school. She insisted you were too young to go, but it was I who persuaded her it was the right thing to do. Life is tough, and the sooner you learn how to cope with it the better for you.'

'What will you tell the school?' I asked him, trembling.

'I'll say you had a very severe infection of the stomach which I am curing with pills,' he answered smiling. 'It will mean that you must stay home for three more days. But promise me you won't try anything like this again. Your mother has enough on her hands without having to rush over to fetch you out of school.'

'I promise,' I said. 'I'll never do it again.'

I'm taking the Calsium, but have'nt needed one of the Pills yet.

A Drive in the Motor-car

Somehow or other I got through the first term at St Peter's, and towards the end of December my mother came over on the paddle-boat to take me and my trunk home for the Christmas holidays.

Dear Mama   Dec 9th

Just to make it a bit planer, I will be coming home on Dec 17th not the 18th. I will drive a Cardiff a four oclock please meet me, if that is not quite planer please noyse let me know what you want to know about it.

Love from Boy.

Oh the bliss and the wonder of being with the family once again after all those weeks of fierce discipline! Unless you have been to boarding-school when you are very young, it is absolutely impossible to appreciate the delights of living at home. It is almost *worth* going away because it's so lovely coming back. I could hardly believe that I didn't have to wash in cold water in the mornings or keep silent in the corridors, or say 'Sir' to every grown-up man I met, or use a chamber-pot in the bedroom, or get flicked with wet towels while naked in the changing-room, or eat porridge for breakfast that seemed full of little round lumpy grey sheep's-droppings, or walk all day long in perpetual fear of the long yellow cane that lay on top of the corner-cupboard in the Headmaster's study.

The weather was exceptionally mild that Christmas holiday and one amazing morning our whole family got ready to go for our first drive in the first motor-car we had ever owned. This new motor-car was an enormous long black French automobile called a De Dion Bouton which had a canvas roof that folded back. The driver was to be that twelve-years-older-than-me half-sister (now aged twenty-one) who had recently had her appendix removed.

She had received two full half-hour lessons in driving from the man who delivered the car, and in that enlightened year of 1925 this was considered quite sufficient. Nobody had to take a driving-test. You were your own judge of competence, and as soon as you felt you were ready to go, off you jolly well went.

As we all climbed into the car, our excitement was so intense we could hardly bear it.

'How fast will it go?' we cried out. 'Will it do fifty miles an hour?'

'It'll do sixty!' the ancient sister answered. Her tone was so confident and cocky it should have scared us to death, but it didn't.

'Oh, let's make it do sixty!' we shouted. 'Will you promise to take us up to sixty?'

'We shall probably go faster than that,' the sister announced, pulling on her driving-gloves and tying a scarf over her head in the approved driving-fashion of the period.

The canvas hood had been folded back because of the mild weather, converting the car into a magnificent open tourer. Up front, there were three bodies in all, the driver behind the wheel, my half-brother (aged eighteen) and one of my sisters (aged twelve). In the back seat there were four more of us, my mother (aged forty), two small sisters (aged eight and five) and myself (aged nine). Our machine possessed one very special feature which I don't think you see on the cars of today. This was a second windscreen in the back solely to keep the breeze off the faces of the back-seat passengers when the hood was down. It had a long centre section and two little end sections that could be angled backwards to deflect the wind.

We were all quivering with fear and joy as the driver let out the clutch and the great long black automobile leaned forward and stole into motion.

'Are you sure you know how to do it?' we shouted. 'Do you know where the brakes are?'

'Be quiet!' snapped the ancient sister. 'I've got to concentrate!'

Down the drive we went and out into the village of Llandaff itself. Fortunately there were very few vehicles on the roads in those days. Occasionally you met a small truck or a delivery-van and now and again a private car, but the danger of colliding with anything else was fairly remote so long as you kept the car on the road.

The splendid black tourer crept slowly through the village with the driver pressing the rubber bulb of the horn every time we passed a human being, whether it was the butcher-boy on his bicycle or just a pedestrian strolling on the pavement. Soon we were entering a countryside of green fields and high hedges with not a soul in sight.

'You didn't think I could do it, did you?' cried the ancient sister, turning round and grinning at us all.

'Now you keep your eyes on the road,' my mother said nervously.

'Go faster!' we shouted. 'Go on! Make her go faster! Put your foot down! We're only doing *fifteen miles an hour!*'

Spurred on by our shouts and taunts, the ancient sister began to increase the speed. The engine roared and the body vibrated. The driver was clutching the steering-wheel as though it were the hair of a drowning man, and we all watched the speedometer needle creeping up to twenty, then twenty-five, then thirty. We were probably doing about thirty-five miles an hour when we came suddenly to a sharpish bend in the road. The ancient sister, never having been faced with a situation like this before, shouted 'Help!' and slammed on the brakes and swung the wheel wildly round. The rear wheels locked and went into a fierce sideways skid, and then, with a marvellous crunch of mudguards and metal, we went crashing into the hedge. The front passengers all shot through the front windscreen and the back passengers all shot through the back windscreen. Glass (there was no Triplex then) flew in all directions and so did we. My brother and one sister landed on the bonnet of the car, someone else was catapulted out on the road and at least one small sister landed in the middle of the hawthorn hedge. But miraculously nobody was hurt very much except me. My nose had been cut almost clean off my face as I went through the rear windscreen and now it was hanging on only by a single small thread of skin. My mother disentangled herself from the scrimmage and grabbed a handkerchief from her purse. She clapped the dangling nose back into place fast and held it there.

Not a cottage or a person was in sight, let alone a telephone. Some kind of bird started twittering in a tree farther down the road, otherwise all was silent.

My mother was bending over me in the rear seat and saying, 'Lean back and keep your head still.' To the ancient sister she said, 'Can you get this thing going again?'

The sister pressed the starter and to everyone's surprise, the engine fired.

'Back it out of the hedge,' my mother said. 'And hurry.'

The sister had trouble finding reverse gear. The cogs were grinding against one another with a fearful noise of tearing metal.

'I've never actually driven it backwards,' she admitted at last.

Everyone with the exception of the driver, my mother and me was out of the car and standing on the road. The noise of gear-wheels grinding against each other was terrible. It sounded as though a lawn-mower was being driven over hard rocks. The ancient sister was using bad words and going crimson in the face, but then my brother leaned his head over the driver's door and said, 'Don't you have to put your foot on the clutch?'

The harassed driver depressed the clutch-pedal and the gears meshed and one second later the great black beast leapt backwards out of the hedge and careered across the road into the hedge on the other side.

'Try to keep cool,' my mother said. 'Go forward slowly.'

At last the shattered motor-car was driven out of the second hedge and stood sideways across the road, blocking the highway. A man with a horse and cart now appeared on the scene and the man dismounted from his cart and walked across to our car and leaned over the rear door. He had a big drooping moustache and he wore a small black bowler-hat.

'You're in a fair old mess 'ere, ain't you?' he said to my mother.

'Can you drive a motor-car?' my mother asked him.

'Nope,' he said. 'And you're blockin' up the 'ole road. I've got a thousand fresh-laid heggs in this cart and I want to get 'em to market before noon.'

'Get out of the way,' my mother told him. 'Can't you see there's a child in here who's badly injured?'

'One thousand fresh-laid heggs,' the man repeated, staring straight at my mother's hand and the blood-soaked handkerchief and the blood running down her wrist. 'And if I don't get 'em to market by noon today I won't be able to sell 'em till next week. Then they won't be fresh-laid any more, will they? I'll be stuck with one thousand stale ole heggs that nobody wants.'

'I hope they all go rotten,' my mother said. 'Now back that cart out of our way this instant!' And to the children standing on the road she cried out, 'Jump back into the car! We're going to the doctor!'

'There's glass all over the seats!' they shouted.

'Never mind the glass!' my mother said. 'We've got to get this boy to the doctor fast!'

The passengers crawled back into the car. The man with the horse and cart backed off to a safe distance. The ancient sister managed to straighten the vehicle and get it pointed in the right direction, and then at last the once magnificent automobile tottered down the highway and headed for Dr Dunbar's surgery in Cathedral Road, Cardiff.

'I've never driven in a city,' the ancient and trembling sister announced.

'You are about to do so,' my mother said. 'Keep going.'

Proceeding at no more than four miles an hour all the way, we finally made it to Dr Dunbar's house. I was hustled out of the car and in through the front door with my mother still holding the bloodstained handkerchief firmly over my wobbling nose.

'Good heavens!' cried Dr Dunbar. 'It's been cut clean off!'

'It hurts,' I moaned.

'He can't go round without a nose for the rest of his life!' the doctor said to my mother.

'It looks as though he may have to,' my mother said.

'Nonsense!' the doctor told her. 'I shall sew it on again.'

'Can you do that?' my mother asked him.

'I can try,' he answered. 'I shall tape it on tight for now and I'll be up at your house with my assistant within the hour.'

Huge strips of sticking plaster were strapped across my face to hold the nose in position. Then I was led back into the car and we crawled the two miles home to Llandaff.

About an hour later I found myself lying upon that same nursery table my ancient sister had occupied some months before for her appendix operation. Strong hands held me down while a mask stuffed with cotton-wool was clamped over my face. I saw a hand above me holding a bottle with white liquid in it and the liquid was being poured on to the cotton wool inside the mask. Once again I smelled the sickly stench of chloroform and ether, and a voice was saying, 'Breathe deeply. Take some nice deep breaths.'

I fought fiercely to get off that table but my shoulders were pinned down by the full weight of a large man. The hand that was holding the bottle above my face kept tilting it farther and farther forward and the white liquid dripped and dripped on to the cotton-wool. Blood red circles began to appear before my eyes and the circles started to spin round and round until they made a scarlet whirlpool with a deep black hole in the centre, and miles away in the distance a voice was saying, 'That's a good boy. We're nearly there now ... we're nearly there ... just close your eyes and go to sleep ...'

I woke up in my own bed with my anxious mother sitting beside me, holding my hand. 'I didn't think you were ever going to come round,' she said. 'You've been asleep for more than eight hours.'

'Did Dr Dunbar sew my nose on again?' I asked her.

'Yes,' she said.

'Will it stay on?'

'He says it will. How do you feel, my darling?'

'Sick,' I said.

After I had vomited into a small basin, I felt a little better.

'Look under your pillow,' my mother said, smiling.

I turned and lifted a corner of my pillow, and underneath it, on the snow-white sheet, there lay a beautiful golden sovereign with the head of King George V on its uppermost side.

'That's for being brave,' my mother said. 'You did very well. I'm proud of you.'

Captain Hardcastle

We called them masters in those days, not teachers, and at St Peter's the one I feared most of all, apart from the Headmaster, was Captain Hardcastle.

This man was slim and wiry and he played football. On the football field he wore white running shorts and white gymshoes and short white socks. His legs were as hard and thin as ram's legs and the skin around his calves was almost exactly the colour of mutton fat. The hair on his head was not ginger. It was brilliant dark vermilion, like a ripe orange, and it was plastered back with immense quantities of brilliantine in the same fashion as the Headmaster's. The parting in his hair was a white line straight down the middle of the scalp, so straight it could only have been made with a ruler. On either side of the parting you could see the comb tracks running back through the greasy orange hair like little tram-lines.

Captain Hardcastle sported a moustache that was the same colour as his hair, and oh what a moustache it was! A truly terrifying sight, a thick orange hedge that sprouted and flourished between his nose and his upper lip and ran clear across his face from the middle of one cheek to the middle of the other. But this was not one of those nailbrush moustaches, all short and clipped and bristly. Nor was it long and droopy in the walrus style. Instead, it was curled most splendidly upwards all the way along as though it had had a permanent wave put into it or possibly curling tongs heated in the mornings over a tiny flame of methylated spirits. The only other way he could have achieved this curling effect, we boys decided, was by prolonged upward brushing with a hard toothbrush in front of the looking-glass every morning.

Behind the moustache there lived an inflamed and savage face with a deeply corrugated brow that indicated a very limited intelligence. 'Life is a puzzlement,' the corrugated brow seemed to be saying, 'and the world is a dangerous place. All men are enemies and small boys are insects that will turn and bite you if you don't get them first and squash them hard.'

Captain Hardcastle was never still. His orange head twitched and jerked perpetually from side to side in the most alarming fashion, and each twitch was accompanied by a little grunt that came out of the nostrils. He had been a soldier in the army in the Great War and that, of course, was how he had received his title. But even small insects like us knew that 'Captain' was not a very exalted rank and only a man with little else to boast about would hang on to it in civilian life. It was bad enough to keep calling yourself 'Major' after it was all over, but 'Captain' was the bottoms.

Rumour had it that the constant twitching and jerking and snorting was caused by something called shell-shock, but we were not quite sure what that was. We took it to mean that an explosive object had gone off very close to him with such an enormous bang that it had made him jump high in the air and he hadn't stopped jumping since.

For a reason that I could never properly understand, Captain Hardcastle had it in for me from my very first day at St Peter's. Perhaps it was because he taught Latin and I was no good at it. Perhaps it was because already, at the age of nine, I was very nearly as tall as he was. Or even more likely, it was because I took an instant dislike to his giant orange moustache and he often caught me staring at it with what was probably a little sneer under the nose. I had only to pass within ten feet of him in the corridor and he would glare at me and shout, 'Hold yourself straight, boy! Pull your shoulders back!' or 'Take those hands out of your pockets!' or 'What's so funny, may I ask? What are you smirking at?' or most insulting of all, '*You*, what's-your-name, get on with your work!' I knew, therefore, that it was only a matter of time before the gallant Captain nailed me good and proper.

The crunch came during my second term when I was exactly nine and a half, and it happened during evening Prep. Every weekday evening, the whole school would sit for one hour in the Main Hall, between six and seven o'clock, to do Prep. The master on duty for the week would be in charge of Prep, which

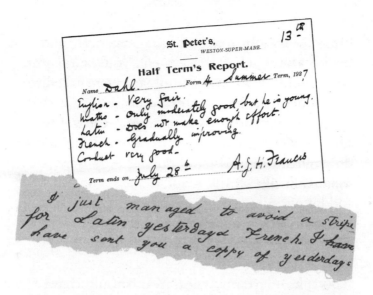

St. Peter's,
WESTON-SUPER-MARE.

Half Term's Report.

Name *Dahl.* Form *4* *Summer* Term, 192*7*

English – *Very fair.*
Maths – *Only moderately good but he is young.*
Latin – *Does not make enough effort.*
French – *Gradually improving.*
Conduct – *very good.*

A. G. H. Francis

Term ends on *July 28*

I just managed to avoid a stripe for Latin yesterday & French. I have sent you a copy of yesterday's

meant that he sat high up on a dais at the top end of the Hall and kept order. Some masters read a book while taking Prep and some corrected exercises, but not Captain Hardcastle. He would sit up there on the dais twitching and grunting and never once would he look down at his desk. His small milky-blue eyes would rove the Hall for the full sixty minutes, searching for trouble, and heaven help the boy who caused it.

The rules of Prep were simple but strict. You were forbidden to look up from your work, and you were forbidden to talk. That was all there was to it, but it left you precious little leeway. In extreme circumstances, and I never knew what these were, you could put your hand up and wait until you were asked to speak but you had better be awfully sure that the circumstances were extreme. Only twice during my four years at St Peter's did I see a boy putting up his hand during Prep. The first one went like this:

MASTER. What is it?

BOY. Please sir, may I be excused to go to the lavatory?

MASTER. Certainly not. You should have gone before.

BOY. But sir . . . please sir . . . I didn't want to go before . . . I didn't know . . .

MASTER. Whose fault was that? Get on with your work!

BOY But sir . . . Oh sir . . . Please sir, let me go!

MASTER. One more word out of you and you'll be in trouble.

Naturally, the wretched boy dirtied his pants, which caused a storm later on upstairs with the Matron.

On the second occasion, I remember clearly

that it was a summer term and the boy who put his hand up was called Braithwaite. I also seem to recollect that the master taking Prep was our friend Captain Hardcastle, but I wouldn't swear to it. The dialogue went something like this:

MASTER. Yes, what is it?

BRAITHWAITE. Please, sir, a wasp came in through the window and it's stung me on my lip and it's swelling up.

MASTER. A *what*?

BRAITHWAITE. A wasp, sir.

MASTER. Speak up, boy, I can't hear you! A *what* came in through the window?

BRAITHWAITE. It's hard to speak up, sir, with my lip all swelling up.

MASTER. With your *what* all swelling up? Are you trying to be funny?

BRAITHWAITE. No sir, I promise I'm not sir.

MASTER. Talk properly, boy! What's the matter with you?

BRAITHWAITE. I've told you, sir. I've been stung, sir. My lip is swelling. It's hurting terribly.

MASTER. *Hurting terribly?* What's hurting terribly?

135

BRAITHWAITE. My lip, sir. It's getting bigger
and bigger.

MASTER. What Prep are you doing tonight?

BRAITHWAITE. French verbs, sir. We have to
write them out.

MASTER. Do you write with your lip?

BRAITHWAITE. No, sir, I don't, sir, but you
see . . .

MASTER. All I see is that you are making an
infernal noise and disturbing everybody in
the room. Now get on with your work.

They were tough, those masters, make no
mistake about it, and if you wanted to survive,
you had to become pretty tough yourself.

My own turn came, as I said, during my
second term and Captain Hardcastle was again
taking Prep. You should know that during
Prep every boy in the Hall sat at his own small
individual wooden desk. These desks had the
usual sloping wooden tops with a narrow
flat strip at the far end where there was a
groove to hold your pen and a small hole in
the right-hand side in which the ink-well sat.
The pens we used had detachable nibs and it
was necessary to dip your nib into the ink-
well every six or seven seconds when you were

writing. Ball-point pens and felt pens had not then been invented, and fountain-pens were forbidden. The nibs we used were very fragile and most boys kept a supply of new ones in a small box in their trouser pockets.

Prep was in progress. Captain Hardcastle was sitting up on the dais in front of us, stroking his orange moustache, twitching his head and grunting through his nose. His eyes roved the Hall endlessly, searching for mischief. The only noises to be heard were Captain Hardcastle's little snorting grunts and the soft sound of pen-nibs moving over paper. Occasionally there was a *ping* as somebody dipped his nib too violently into his tiny white porcelain ink-well.

Disaster struck when I foolishly stubbed the tip of my nib into the top of the desk. The nib broke. I knew I hadn't got a spare one in my pocket, but a broken nib was never accepted as an excuse for not finishing Prep. We had been set an essay to write and the subject was 'The Life Story of a Penny' (I still have that essay in my files). I had made a decent start and I was rattling along fine when I broke that nib. There was still another half-hour of Prep to go and I couldn't sit there doing nothing all that time.

Nor could I put up my hand and tell Captain Hardcastle I had broken my nib. I simply did not dare. And as a matter of fact, I really *wanted* to finish that essay. I knew exactly what was going to happen to my penny through the next two pages and I couldn't bear to leave it unsaid.

in the gutter. Down, ... muddy water. The drain went into a went flowed rapidly on. Into this river I was washed, gone down with the current and after having washed down a considerable distance. I found myself washed high and dry on the bank. Then two boys came along, & the smallest one saw me for

I glanced to my right. The boy next to me was called Dobson. He was the same age as me, nine and a half, and a nice fellow. Even now, sixty years later, I can still remember that Dobson's father was a doctor and that he lived, as I had learnt from the label on Dobson's tuck-box, at The Red House, Uxbridge, Middlesex.

Dobson's desk was almost touching mine. I thought I would risk it. I kept my head lowered but watched Captain Hardcastle very carefully.

When I was fairly sure he was looking the other way, I put a hand in front of my mouth and whispered, 'Dobson . . . Dobson . . . Could you lend me a nib?'

Suddenly there was an explosion up on the dais. Captain Hardcastle had leapt to his feet and was pointing at me and shouting, 'You're talking! I saw you talking! Don't try to deny it! I distinctly saw you talking behind your hand!'

I sat there frozen with terror.

Every boy stopped working and looked up.

Captain Hardcastle's face had gone from red to deep purple and he was twitching violently.

'Do you deny you were talking?' he shouted.

'No, sir, no, b-but . . .'

'And do you deny you were trying to cheat? Do you deny you were asking Dobson for help with your work?'

'N-no, sir, I wasn't. I wasn't cheating.'

'Of course you were cheating! Why else, may I ask, would you be speaking to Dobson? I take it you were not inquiring after his health?'

It is worth reminding the reader once again of my age. I was not a self-possessed lad of fourteen. Nor was I twelve or even ten years old. I was nine and a half, and at that age one is ill equipped to tackle a grown-up man with flaming orange hair and a violent temper. One can do little else but stutter.

'I . . . I have broken my nib, sir,' I whispered. 'I . . . I was asking Dobson if he c-could lend me one, sir.'

'You are lying!' cried Captain Hardcastle, and there was triumph in his voice. 'I always knew you were a liar! *And* a cheat as well!'

'All I w-wanted was a nib, sir.'

'I'd shut up if I were you!' thundered the voice on the dais. 'You'll only get yourself into deeper trouble! I am giving you a Stripe!'

These were words of doom. A Stripe! *I am giving you a Stripe!* All around, I could feel a kind of sympathy reaching out to me from every boy in the school, but nobody moved or made a sound.

Here I must explain the system of Stars and Stripes that we had at St Peter's. For exceptionally good work, you could be awarded a Quarter-Star, and a red dot was made with crayon beside your name on the notice-board. If you got four Quarter-Stars, a red line was drawn through the four dots indicating that you had completed your Star.

For exceptionally poor work or bad behaviour, you were given a Stripe, and that automatically meant a thrashing from the Headmaster.

Every master had a book of Quarter-Stars and a book of Stripes, and these had to be filled in and signed and torn out exactly like cheques from a cheque book. The Quarter-Stars were pink, the Stripes were a fiendish, blue-green colour. The boy who received a Star or a Stripe would pocket it until the following morning after prayers, when the Headmaster would call upon anyone who had been given one or the other to come forward in front of the whole school and hand it in. Stripes were considered so dreadful that they were not given very often. In any one week it was unusual for more than two or three boys to receive Stripes.

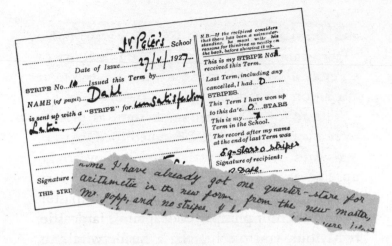

And now Captain Hardcastle was giving one to me.

'Come here,' he ordered.

I got up from my desk and walked to the dais. He already had his book of Stripes on the desk and was filling one out. He was using red ink, and along the line where it said *Reason*, he wrote, *Talking in Prep, trying to cheat and lying*. He signed it and tore it out of the book. Then, taking plenty of time, he filled in the counterfoil. He picked up the terrible piece of green-blue paper and waved it in my direction but he didn't look up. I took it out of his hand and walked back to my desk. The eyes of the whole school followed my progress.

For the remainder of Prep I sat at my desk

and did nothing. Having no nib, I was unable to write another word about 'The Life Story of a Penny', but I was made to finish it the next afternoon instead of playing games.

The following morning, as soon as prayers were over, the Headmaster called for Quarter-Stars and Stripes. I was the only boy to go up. The assistant masters were sitting on very upright chairs on either side of the Headmaster, and I caught a glimpse of Captain Hardcastle, arms folded across his chest, head twitching, the milky-blue eyes watching me intently, the look of triumph still glimmering on his face. I handed in my Stripe. The Headmaster took it and read the writing. 'Come and see me in my study,' he said, 'as soon as this is over.'

Five minutes later, walking on my toes and trembling terribly, I passed through the green baize door and entered the sacred precincts where the Headmaster lived. I knocked on his study door.

'Enter!'

I turned the knob and went into this large square room with bookshelves and easy chairs and the gigantic desk topped in red leather straddling the far corner. The Headmaster was sitting behind the desk holding my Stripe in his fingers. 'What have you got to say for yourself?' he asked me, and the white shark's teeth flashed dangerously between his lips.

'I didn't lie, sir,' I said. 'I promise I didn't. And I wasn't trying to cheat.'

'Captain Hardcastle says you were doing both,' the Headmaster said. 'Are you calling Captain Hardcastle a liar?'

'No, sir. Oh no, sir.'

'I wouldn't if I were you.'

'I had broken my nib, sir, and I was asking Dobson if he could lend me another.'

'That is not what Captain Hardcastle says. He says you were asking for help with your essay.'

'Oh no, sir, I wasn't. I was a long way away from Captain Hardcastle and I was only whispering. I don't think he could have heard what I said, sir.'

'So you *are* calling him a liar.'

'Oh no, sir! No, sir! I would never do that!'

It was impossible for me to win against the Headmaster. What I would like to have said was, 'Yes, sir, if you really want to know, sir, I *am* calling Captain Hardcastle a liar because that's what he is!', but it was out of the question. I did, however, have one trump card left to play, or I thought I did.

'You could ask Dobson, sir,' I whispered.

'*Ask Dobson?*' he cried. 'Why should I ask Dobson?'

'He could tell you what I said, sir.'

'Captain Hardcastle is an officer and a gentleman,' the Headmaster said. 'He has told me what happened. I hardly think I want to go round asking some silly little boy if Captain Hardcastle is speaking the truth.'

I kept silent.

'For talking in Prep,' the Headmaster went on, 'for trying to cheat and for lying, I am going to give you six strokes of the cane.'

He rose from his desk and crossed over to the corner cupboard on the opposite side of the study. He reached up and took from the top of it three very thin yellow canes, each with the bent-over handle at one end. For a few seconds, he held them in his hands, examining them with some care, then he selected one and replaced the other two on top of the cupboard.

'Bend over.'

the cane again

I was frightened of that cane. There is no small boy in the world who wouldn't be. It wasn't simply an instrument for beating you. It was a weapon for wounding. It lacerated the skin. It caused severe black and scarlet bruising that took three weeks to disappear, and all the time during those three weeks, you could feel your heart beating along the wounds.

I tried once more, my voice slightly hysterical now. 'I didn't do it, sir! I swear I'm telling the truth!'

'Be quiet and bend over! Over there! And touch your toes!'

Very slowly, I bent over. Then I shut my eyes and braced for the first stroke.

Crack! It was like a rifle shot! With a very hard stroke of the cane on one's buttocks, the time-lag before you feel any pain is about four seconds. Thus, the experienced caner will always pause between strokes to allow the agony to reach its peak.

So for a few seconds after the first *crack* I felt virtually nothing. Then suddenly came the frightful searing agonizing unbearable burning across the buttocks, and as it reached its highest and most excruciating point, the second *crack* came down. I clutched hold of my ankles as tight as I could and I bit into my lower lip. I was determined not to make a sound, for that would only give the executioner greater satisfaction.

Crack! . . . Five seconds pause.

Crack! . . . Another pause.

Crack! . . . And another pause.

I was counting the strokes, and as the sixth one hit me, I knew I was going to survive in silence.

'That will do,' the voice behind me said.

I straightened up and clutched my backside as hard as I possibly could with both hands. This is always the instinctive and automatic reaction. The pain is so frightful you try to grab hold of it and tear it away, and the tighter you squeeze, the more it helps.

I did not look at the Headmaster as I hopped across the thick red carpet towards the door. The door was closed and nobody was about to open it for me, so for a couple of seconds I had to let go of my bottom with one hand to turn the door-knob. Then I was out and hopping around in the hallway of the private sanctum.

Directly across the hall from the Headmaster's study was the assistant masters' Common Room. They were all in there now waiting to spread out to their respective classrooms, but what I couldn't help noticing, even in my agony, was that *this door was open.*

Why was it open?

Had it been left that way on purpose so that they could all hear more clearly the sound of the cane from across the hall?

Of course it had. And I felt quite sure that it was Captain Hardcastle who had opened it. I pictured him standing in there among his colleagues snorting with satisfaction at every stinging stroke.

Small boys can be very comradely when a member of their community has got into trouble, and even more so when they feel an injustice has been done. When I returned to the classroom, I was surrounded on all sides by sympathetic faces and voices, but one particular incident has always stayed with me. A boy of my own age called Highton was so violently incensed by the whole affair that he said to me before lunch that day, '*You* don't have a father. I do. I am going to write to my father and tell him what has happened and he'll do something about it.'

'He couldn't do anything,' I said.

'Oh yes he could,' Highton said. 'And what's

more he will. My father won't let them get away with this.'

'Where is he now?'

'He's in Greece,' Highton said. 'In Athens. But that won't make any difference.'

Then and there, little Highton sat down and wrote to the father he admired so much, but of course nothing came of it. It was nevertheless a touching and generous gesture from one small boy to another and I have never forgotten it.

Little Ellis and the Boil

During my third term at St Peter's, I got flu and was put to bed in the Sick Room, where the dreaded Matron reigned supreme. In the next bed to mine was a seven-year-old boy called Ellis, whom I liked a lot. Ellis was there because he had an immense and angry-looking boil on the inside of his thigh. I saw it. It was as big as a plum and about the same colour.

One morning, in came the doctor to examine us, and sailing along beside him was the Matron. Her mountainous bosom was enclosed in a starched white envelope, and because of this she somehow reminded me of a painting I had once seen of a four-masted scooner in full canvas running before the wind.

'What's his temperature today?' the doctor asked, pointing at me.

'Just over a hundred, doctor,' the Matron told him.

'He's been up here long enough,' the doctor said. 'Send him back to school tomorrow.' Then he turned to Ellis. 'Take off your pyjama trousers,' he said. He was a very small doctor, with steel-rimmed spectacles and a bald head. He frightened the life out of me.

Ellis removed his pyjama trousers. The doctor bent forward and looked at the boil. 'Hmmm,' he said. 'That's a nasty one, isn't it? We're going to have to do something about that, aren't we, Ellis?'

'What are you going to do?' Ellis asked, trembling.

'Nothing for you to worry about,' the doctor said. 'Just lie back and take no notice of me.'

Little Ellis lay back with his head on the

pillow. The doctor had put his bag on the floor at the end of Ellis's bed, and now he knelt down on the floor and opened the bag. Ellis, even when he lifted his head from the pillow, couldn't see what the doctor was doing there. He was hidden by the end of the bed. But I saw everything. I saw him take out a sort of scalpel which had a long steel handle and a small pointed blade. He crouched below the end of Ellis's bed, holding the scalpel in his right hand.

'Give me a large towel, Matron,' he said.

The Matron handed him a towel.

Still crouching low and hidden from little Ellis's view by the end of the bed, the doctor unfolded the towel and spread it over the palm of his left hand. In his right hand he held the scalpel.

Ellis was frightened and suspicious. He started raising himself up on his elbows to get a better look. 'Lie down, Ellis,' the doctor said, and even as he spoke, he bounced up from the end of the bed like a jack-in-the-box and flung the outspread towel straight into Ellis's face. Almost in the same second, he thrust his right arm forward and plunged the point of the scalpel deep into the centre of the enormous boil. He gave the blade a quick twist and then withdrew it again before the wretched boy had had time to disentangle his head from the towel.

Ellis screamed. He never saw the scalpel going in and he never saw it coming out, but he felt it all right and he screamed like a stuck pig. I can see him now struggling to get the towel off his head, and when he emerged the tears were streaming down his cheeks and his huge brown eyes were staring at the doctor with a look of utter and total outrage.

'Don't make such a fuss about nothing,' the Matron said.

'Put a dressing on it, Matron,' the doctor said, 'with plenty of mag sulph paste.' And he marched out of the room.

I couldn't really blame the doctor. I thought he handled things rather cleverly. Pain was something we were expected to endure. Anaesthetics and pain-killing injections were not much used in those days. Dentists, in particular, never bothered with them. But I doubt very much if you would be entirely happy today if a doctor threw a towel in your face and jumped on you with a knife.

the wart on my thum has come off beautifly, but the one on my knee hasn't even turned into a blister.
You meant me to learn singing didnt you.

Goat's Tobacco

When I was about nine, the ancient half-sister got engaged to be married. The man of her choice was a young English doctor and that summer he came with us to Norway. Romance was floating in the air like moondust and the two lovers, for some reason we younger ones could never understand, did not seem to be very keen on us tagging along with them. They went out in the boat alone. They climbed the rocks alone. They even had breakfast alone.

manly lover and ancient half-sister (in background)

We resented this. As a family we had always done everything together and we didn't see why the ancient half-sister should suddenly decide to do things differently even if she had become engaged. We were inclined to blame the male lover for disrupting the calm of our family life, and it was inevitable that he would have to suffer for it sooner or later.

The male lover was a great pipe-smoker. The disgusting smelly pipe was never out of his mouth except when he was eating or swimming. We even began to wonder whether he removed it when he was kissing his betrothed. He gripped the stem of the pipe in the most manly fashion between his strong white teeth and kept it there while talking to you. This annoyed us. Surely it was more polite to take it out and speak properly.

One day, we all went in our little motor-boat to an island we had never been to before, and for once the ancient half-sister and the manly lover decided to come with us. We chose this particular island because we saw some goats on it. They were climbing about on the rocks and we thought it would be fun to go and visit them. But when we landed, we found that the goats were totally wild and we couldn't get near them. So we gave up trying to make friends with them and simply sat around on the smooth rocks in our bathing costumes, enjoying the lovely sun.

The manly lover was filling his pipe. I happened to be watching him as he very carefully packed the tobacco into the bowl from a yellow oilskin pouch. He had just finished doing this and was about to light up when the ancient half-sister called on him to come swimming. So he put down the pipe and off he went.

I stared at the pipe that was lying there on the rocks. About twelve inches away from it, I saw a little heap of dried goat's droppings, each one small and round like a pale brown berry, and at that point, an interesting idea began to sprout in my mind. I picked up the pipe and knocked all the tobacco out of it. I then took the goat's droppings and teased them with my fingers until they were nicely shredded. Very gently I poured these shredded droppings into the bowl of the pipe, packing them down with my thumb just as the manly lover always did it. When that was done, I placed a thin layer of real tobacco over the top. The entire family was watching me as I did this. Nobody said a word, but I could sense a glow of approval all round. I replaced the pipe on the rock, and all of us sat back to await the return of the victim. The whole lot of us were in this together now, even my mother. I had drawn them into the plot simply by letting them see what I was doing. It was a silent, rather dangerous family conspiracy.

Back came the manly lover, dripping wet from the sea, chest out, strong and virile, healthy and sunburnt. 'Great swim!' he announced to the world. 'Splendid water! Terrific stuff!' He towelled himself vigorously, making the muscles of his biceps ripple, then he sat down on the rocks and reached for his pipe.

Nine pairs of eyes watched him intently. Nobody giggled to give the game away. We were trembling with anticipation, and a good deal of the suspense was caused by the fact that none of us knew just what was going to happen.

The manly lover put the pipe between his strong white teeth and struck a match. He held the flame over the bowl and sucked. The tobacco ignited and glowed, and the lover's head was enveloped in clouds of blue smoke. 'Ah-h-h,' he said, blowing smoke through his nostrils. 'There's nothing like a good pipe after a bracing swim.'

Still we waited. We could hardly bear the

suspense. The sister who was seven couldn't bear it at all. 'What *sort* of tobacco do you put in that thing?' she asked with superb innocence.

'Navy Cut,' the male lover answered. 'Player's Navy Cut. It's the best there is. These Norwegians use all sorts of disgusting scented tobaccos, but I wouldn't touch them.'

'I didn't know they had different tastes,' the small sister went on.

'Of course they do,' the manly lover said. 'All tobaccos are different to the discriminating pipe-smoker. Navy Cut is clean and unadulter-ated. It's a man's smoke.' The man seemed to go out of his way to use long words like discriminating and unadulterated. We hadn't the foggiest what they meant.

The ancient half-sister, fresh from her swim

and now clothed in a towel bathrobe, came and sat herself close to her manly lover. Then the two of them started giving each other those silly little glances and soppy smiles that made us all feel sick. They were far too occupied with one another to notice the awful tension that had settled over our group. They didn't even notice that every face in the crowd was turned towards them. They had sunk once again into their lovers' world where little children did not exist.

The sea was calm, the sun was shining and it was a beautiful day.

Then all of a sudden, the manly lover let out a piercing scream and his whole body shot about four feet into the air. His pipe flew out of his mouth and went clattering over the rocks, and the second scream he gave was so shrill and loud that all the seagulls on the island rose up in alarm. His features were twisted like those of a person undergoing severe torture, and his skin had turned the colour of snow. He began spluttering and choking and spewing and hawking and acting generally like a man with some serious internal injury. He was completely speechless.

We started at him, enthralled.

The ancient half-sister, who must have

thought she was about to lose her future husband
for ever, was pawing at him and thumping him
on the back and crying, 'Darling! Darling!
What's happening to you? Where does it hurt?
Get the boat! Start the engine! We must rush
him to a hospital quickly!' She seemed to have
forgotten that there wasn't a hospital within
fifty miles.

'I've been poisoned!' spluttered the manly
lover. 'It's got into my lungs! It's in my chest!
My chest is on fire! My stomach's going up in
flames!'

'Help me get him into the boat! Quick!'
cried the ancient half-sister, gripping him
under the armpits. 'Don't just sit there staring!
Come and help!'

'No, no, no!' cried the now not-so-manly
lover. 'Leave me alone! I need air! Give me air!'
He lay back and breathed in deep draughts of
splendid Norwegian ocean air, and in another
minute or so, he was sitting up again and was
on the way to recovery.

'What in the world came over you?' asked
the ancient half-sister, clasping his hands
tenderly in hers.

'I can't imagine,' he murmured. 'I simply
can't imagine.' His face was as still and white

as virgin snow and his hands were trembling. 'There must be a reason for it,' he added. 'There's got to be a reason.'

'I know the reason!' shouted the seven-year-old sister, screaming with laughter. 'I know what it was!'

'What was it?' snapped the ancient one. 'What have you been up to? Tell me at once!'

'It's his pipe!' shouted the small sister, still convulsed with laughter.

'What's wrong with my pipe?' said the manly lover.

'You've been smoking goat's tobacco!' cried the small sister.

It took a few moments for the full meaning of these words to dawn upon the two lovers, but when it did, and when the terrible anger began to show itself on the manly lover's face, and when he started to rise slowly and menacingly to his feet, we all sprang up and ran for our lives and jumped off the rocks into the deep water.

Repton and Shell, 1929–36

(age 13–20)

THE PRIORY HOUSE,
REPTON,
DERBY.

Dear Mema

Thanks awfully for the parcel
and your letters. We had a great supper
last night. We fried the sausages and poured
hieny beans over them. then we had force &
cream. Those biscuits are awfully good.
Last night we had a heavy snowfall, and
there is about ___ of snow on the ground.
Tobogganing
macdonald & J ___

Love Ro

Ronald

on ship to Newfoundland
1933

photography at Repton

Getting Dressed for
the Big School

When I was twelve, my mother said to me, 'I've entered you for Marlborough and Repton. Which would you like to go to?'

Both were famous Public Schools, but that was all I knew about them. 'Repton,' I said. 'I'll go to Repton.' It was an easier word to say than Marlborough.

'Very well,' my mother said. 'You shall go to Repton.'

We were living in Kent then, in a place called Bexley. Repton was up in the Midlands, near Derby and some 140 miles away to the north. This was of no consequence. There were plenty of trains. Nobody was taken to school by car in those days. We were put on the train.

alfhild, me, asta, Else
and dogs. Tenby.

I was exactly thirteen in September 1929 when the time came for me to go to Repton. On the day of my departure, I had first of all to get dressed for the part. I had been to London with my mother the week before to buy the school clothes, and I remember how shocked I was when I saw the outfit I was expected to wear.

'I can't possibly go about in *those!*' I cried. 'Nobody wears things like that!'

'Are you sure you haven't made a mistake?' my mother said to the shop assistant.

'If he's going to Repton, madam, he must wear these clothes,' the assistant said firmly.

And now this amazing fancy-dress was all laid out on my bed waiting to be put on. 'Put it on,' my mother said. 'Hurry up or you'll miss the train.'

'I'll look like a complete idiot,' I said. My mother went out of the room and left me to it. With immense reluctance, I began to dress myself.

First there was a white shirt with a detachable white collar. This collar was unlike any other collar I had seen. It was as stiff as a piece of perspex. At the front, the stiff points of the collar were bent over to make a pair of wings, and the whole thing was so tall that the points of the wings, as I discovered later, rubbed against the underneath of my chin. It was known as a butterfly collar.

To attach the butterfly collar to the shirt you needed a back stud and a front stud. I had never been through this rigmarole before. I must do this properly, I told myself. So first I put the back stud into the back of the collar-band of the shirt. Then I tried to attach the back of the collar to the back stud, but the collar was so stiff I couldn't get the stud through the slit. I decided to soften it with spit. I put the edge of the collar into my mouth and sucked the starch away. It worked. The stud went through the slit and the back of the collar was now attached to the back of the shirt.

I inserted the front stud into one side of the front of the shirt and slipped the shirt over my head. With the help of a mirror, I now set about pushing the top of the front stud through the first of the two slits in the front of the collar. It wouldn't go. The slit was so small and stiff and starchy that nothing would go through it. I took the shirt off and put both the front slits of the collar into my mouth and chewed them until they were soft. The starch didn't taste of anything. I put the shirt back on again and at last I was able to get the front stud through the collar-slits.

Around the collar but underneath the butterfly wings, I tied a black tie, using an ordinary tie-knot.

Dear mama
Thanks for your letter.
I mean half a dozen Van Heusen Collars. not Shirts.
Love for
Roald?

Then came the trousers and the braces. The trousers were black with thin pinstriped grey lines running down them. I buttoned the braces on to the trousers, six buttons in all, then I put on the trousers and adjusted the braces to the correct length by sliding two brass clips up and down.

I put on a brand new pair of black shoes and laced them up.

Now for the waistcoat. This was also black and it had twelve buttons down the front and two little waistcoat pockets on either side, one above the other. I put it on and did up the buttons, starting at the top and working down. I was glad I didn't have to chew each of those button-holes to get the buttons through them.

All this was bad enough for a boy who had never before worn anything more elaborate than a pair of shorts and a blazer. But the jacket put the lid on it. It wasn't actually a jacket, it was a sort of tail-coat, and it was without a doubt the most ridiculous garment I had ever seen.

Like the waistcoat, it was jet black and made of a heavy serge-like material. In the front it was cut away so that the two sides met only at one point, about halfway down the waistcoat. Here there was a single button and this had to be done up. From the button downwards, the lines of the coat separated and curved away behind the legs of the wearer and came together again at the backs of the knees, forming a pair of 'tails'. These tails were separated by a slit and when you walked about they flapped against your legs. I put the thing on and did up the front button. Feeling like an undertaker's apprentice in a funeral parlour, I crept downstairs.

My sisters shrieked with laughter when I appeared. 'He can't go out in *those*!' they cried. 'He'll be arrested by the police.'

the hat-band being & something like this: ——————— , the white stripes are realy blue, and the bit filled in is black. f. th.

'Put your hat on,' my mother said, handing me a stiff wide-brimmed straw-hat with a blue and black band around it. I put it on and did my best to look dignified. The sisters fell all over the room laughing.

My mother got me out of the house before
I lost my nerve completely and together we
walked through the village to Bexley station.
My mother was going to accompany me to
London and see me on to the Derby train, but
she had been told that on no account should
she travel farther than that. I had only a small
suitcase to carry. My trunk had been sent on
ahead labelled 'Luggage in Advance'.

'Nobody's taking the slightest notice of you,'
my mother said as we walked through Bexley
High Street.

And curiously enough nobody was.

'I have learnt one thing about England,' my
mother went on. 'It is a country where men
love to wear uniforms and eccentric clothes.
Two hundred years ago their clothes were even
more eccentric than they are today. You can

consider yourself lucky you don't have to wear a wig on your head and ruffles on your sleeves.'

'I still feel an ass,' I said.

'Everyone who looks at you,' my mother said, 'knows that you are going away to a Public School. All English Public Schools have their own different crazy uniforms. People will be thinking how lucky you are to be going to one of those famous places.'

We took the train from Bexley to Charing Cross and then went by taxi to Euston Station. At Euston, I was put on the train for Derby with a lot of other boys who all wore the same ridiculous clothes as me, and away I went.

Beagling, Repton 1930.

Boazers

At Repton, prefects were never called prefects. They were called Boazers, and they had the power of life and death over us junior boys. They could summon us down in our pyjamas at night-time and thrash us for leaving just one football sock on the floor of the changing-room when it should have been hung up on a peg. A Boazer could thrash us for a hundred and one other piddling little misdemeanours – for burning his toast at tea-time, for failing to dust his study properly, for failing to get his study fire burning in spite of spending half your pocket money on fire-lighters, for being late at roll-call, for talking in evening Prep, for forgetting to change into house-shoes at six o'clock. The list was endless.

'Four with the dressing-gown on or three with it off?' the Boazer would say to you in the changing-room late at night.

Others in the dormitory had told you what to answer to this question. 'Four with it on,' you mumbled, trembling.

This Boazer was famous for the speed of his strokes. Most of them paused between each stroke to prolong the operation, but Williamson, the great footballer, cricketer and athlete, always delivered his strokes in a series of swift back and forth movements without any pause between them at all. Four strokes would rain down upon your bottom so fast that it was all over in four seconds.

A ritual took place in the dormitory after each beating. The victim was required to stand in the middle of the room and lower his pyjama trousers so that the damage could be inspected. Half a dozen experts would crowd round you and express their opinions in highly professional language.

'*What* a super job.'

'He's got *every single* one in the same place!'

'Crikey! Nobody could tell you had had more than *one*, except for the mess!'

'Boy, that Williamson's got a *terrific* eye!'

'*Of course* he's got a terrific eye! Why d'you think he's a Cricket Teamer?'

'There's no wet blood though! If you had had just one more he'd have got some blood out!'

'Through a *dressing-gown*, too! It's pretty amazing, isn't it!'

'Most Boazers couldn't get a result like that *without* a dressing-gown!'

'You must have tremendously thin skin! Even Williamson couldn't have done that to *ordinary* skin!'

'Did he use the long one or the short one?'

'Hang *on*! Don't pull them up yet! I've *got* to see this again!'

And I would stand there, slightly bemused by this cool clinical approach. Once, I was still standing in the middle of the dormitory with my pyjama trousers around my knees when Williamson came through the door. 'What on earth do you think you're doing?' he said, knowing very well exactly what I was doing.

'N-nothing,' I stammered. 'N-nothing at all.'

'Pull those pyjamas up and get into bed immediately!' he ordered but I noticed that as he turned away to go out of the door, he craned his head ever so slightly to one side to catch a glimpse of my bare bottom and his own handiwork. I was certain I detected a little glimmer of pride around the edges of his mouth before he closed the door behind him.

The Headmaster

and again!

The Headmaster, while I was at Repton, struck me as being a rather shoddy bandy-legged little fellow with a big bald head and lots of energy but not much charm. Mind you, I never did know him well because in all those months and years I was at the school, I doubt whether he addressed more than six sentences to me altogether. So perhaps it was wrong of me to form a judgement like that.

What is so interesting about this Headmaster is that he became a famous person later on. At the end of my third year, he was suddenly appointed Bishop of Chester and off he went to live in a palace by the River Dee. I remember at the time trying to puzzle out how on earth a person could suddenly leap from being a schoolmaster to becoming a Bishop all in one jump, but there were bigger puzzles to come.

From Chester, he was soon promoted again to become Bishop of London, and from there, after not all that many years, he bounced up the ladder once more to get the top job of them all, Archbishop of Canterbury! And not long after that it was he himself who had the task of crowning our present Queen in Westminster Abbey with half the world watching him on television. Well, well, well! And this was the man who used to deliver the most vicious beatings to the boys under his care!

By now I am sure you will be wondering why I lay so much emphasis upon school beatings in these pages. The answer is that I cannot help it. All through my school life I was appalled by the fact that masters and senior boys were allowed literally to wound other boys, and sometimes quite severely. I couldn't get over it. I never have got over it. It would, of course, be unfair to suggest that *all* masters were constantly beating the daylights out of *all* the boys in those days. They weren't. Only a few did so, but that was quite enough to leave a lasting impression of horror upon me. It left another more physical impression upon me as well. Even today, when-ever I have to sit for any length of time on a hard bench or chair, I begin to feel my heart beating along the lines that the cane made on my bottom some fifty-five years ago.

There is nothing wrong with a few quick

sharp tickles on the rump. They probably do a naughty boy a lot of good. But this Headmaster we were talking about wasn't just tickling you when he took out his cane to deliver a flogging. He never flogged me, thank goodness, but I was given a vivid description of one of these ceremonies by my best friend at Repton, whose name was Michael. Michael was ordered to take down his trousers and kneel on the Headmaster's sofa with the top half of his body hanging over one end of the sofa. The great man then gave him one terrific crack. After that, there was a pause. The cane was put down and the Headmaster began filling his pipe from a tin of tobacco. He also started to lecture the kneeling boy about sin and wrongdoing. Soon, the cane was picked up again and a second tremendous crack was administered upon the trembling buttocks. Then the pipe-filling business and the lecture went on for maybe another thirty seconds. Then came the third crack of the cane. Then the instrument of torture was put once more upon the table and a box of matches was produced. A match was struck and applied to the pipe. The pipe failed to light properly. A fourth stroke was delivered, with the lecture continuing. This slow and fearsome process went on until ten terrible strokes had been delivered, and all the time, over the pipe-lighting and the match-striking, the lecture on evil and wrongdoing and sinning and misdeeds and malpractice went on without a stop. It even went on as the strokes were being administered. At the end of it all, a basin, a sponge and a small clean towel were produced by the Headmaster, and the victim was told to wash away the blood before pulling up his trousers.

Do you wonder then that this man's behaviour used to puzzle me tremendously? He was an ordinary clergyman at that time as well as being a Headmaster, and I would sit in the dim light of the school chapel and listen to him preaching about the Lamb of God and about Mercy and Forgiveness and all the rest of it and my young mind would become totally confused. I knew very well that only the night before this preacher had shown neither Forgiveness nor Mercy in flogging some small boy who had broken the rules.

So what was it all about? I used to ask myself.

Did they preach one thing and practise another, these men of God?

And if someone had told me at the time that

this flogging clergyman was one day to become the Archbishop of Canterbury, I would never have believed it.

It was all this, I think, that made me begin to have doubts about religion and even about God. If this person, I kept telling myself, was one of God's chosen salesmen on earth, then there must be something very wrong about the whole business.

Chocolates

Every now and then, a plain grey cardboard box was dished out to each boy in our House, and this, believe it or not, was a present from the great chocolate manufacturers, Cadbury. Inside the box there were twelve bars of chocolate, all of different shapes, all with different fillings and all with numbers from one to twelve stamped on the chocolate underneath. Eleven of these bars were new inventions from the factory. The twelfth was the 'control' bar, one that we all knew well, usually a Cadbury's Coffee Cream bar. Also in the box was a sheet of paper with the numbers one to twelve on it as well as two blank columns, one for giving marks to each chocolate from nought to ten, and the other for comments.

All we were required to do in return for this splendid gift was to taste very carefully each bar of chocolate, give it marks and make an intelligent comment on why we liked it or disliked it.

It was a clever stunt. Cadbury's were using some of the greatest chocolate-bar experts in the world to test out their new inventions.

We were of a sensible age, between thirteen and eighteen, and we knew intimately every chocolate bar in existence, from the Milk Flake to the Lemon Marshmallow. Quite obviously our opinions on anything new would be valuable. All of us entered into this game with great gusto, sitting in our studies and nibbling each bar with the air of connoisseurs, giving our marks and making our comments. 'Too subtle for the common palate,' was one note that I remember writing down.

For me, the importance of all this was that I began to realize that the large chocolate companies actually did possess inventing rooms and they took their inventing very seriously. I used to picture a long white room like a laboratory with pots of chocolate and fudge and all sorts of other delicious fillings bubbling away on the stoves, while men and women in white coats moved between the bubbling pots, tasting and mixing and concocting their wonderful new inventions. I used to imagine myself working in one of these labs and suddenly I would come up with something so absolutely unbearably delicious that I would grab it in my hand and go rushing out of the lab and along the corridor and right into the office of the great Mr Cadbury himself. 'I've got it, sir!' I would shout, putting the chocolate in front of him. 'It's fantastic! It's fabulous! It's marvellous! It's irresistible!'

Slowly, the great man would pick up my newly invented chocolate and he would take a small bite. He would roll it round his mouth. Then all at once, he would leap from his chair, crying, 'You've got it! You've done it! It's a miracle!' He would slap me on the back and shout, 'We'll sell it by the million! We'll sweep the world with this one! How on earth did you do it? Your salary is doubled!'

It was lovely dreaming those dreams, and I have no doubt at all that, thirty-five years later, when I was looking for a plot for my second book for children, I remembered those little cardboard boxes and the newly-invented chocolates inside them, and I began to write a book called *Charlie and the Chocolate Factory*.

Saturday, first I broke it in half, and only half came out, then the other bit came out, it was my dog tooth, and it was a very bad one, I am glad it came out. Will you please send me a few sweets because we had none, last week, I am sorry my writing is so untidy, but I have not much time on week Days.

Corkers

There were about thirty or more masters at Repton and most of them were amazingly dull and totally colourless and completely uninterested in boys. But Corkers, an eccentric old bachelor, was neither dull nor colourless. Corkers was a charmer, a vast ungainly man with drooping bloodhound cheeks and filthy clothes. He wore creaseless flannel trousers and a brown tweed jacket with patches all over it and bits of dried food on the lapels. He was meant to teach us mathematics, but in truth he taught us nothing at all and that was the way he meant it to be. His lessons consisted of an endless series of distractions all invented by him so that the subject of mathematics would never have to be discussed. He would come lumbering into the classroom and sit down at his desk and glare at the class. We would wait expectantly, wondering what was coming next.

'Let's have a look at the crossword puzzle in today's *Times*,' he would say, fishing a crumpled newspaper out of his jacket pocket. 'That'll be a lot more fun than fiddling around with figures. I hate figures. Figures are probably the dreariest things on this earth.'

'Then why do you teach mathematics, sir?' somebody asked him.

'I don't,' he said, smiling slyly. 'I only *pretend* to teach it.'

Corkers would proceed to draw the framework of the crossword on the blackboard and we would all spend the rest of the lesson trying to solve it while he read out the clues. We enjoyed that.

The only time I can remember him vaguely touching upon mathematics was when he whisked a square of tissue-paper out of his pocket and waved it around. 'Look at this,' he said. 'This tissue-paper is one-hundredth of an inch thick. I fold it once, making it double. I fold it again, making it four thicknesses. Now then, I will give a large bar of Cadbury's Fruit and Nut Milk Chocolate to any boy who can tell me, to the nearest twelve inches, how thick it will be if I fold it fifty times.'

We all stuck up our hands and started guessing. 'Twenty-four inches, sir' ... 'Three feet, sir' ... 'Five yards, sir' ... 'Three inches, sir.'

'You're not very clever, are you,' Corkers said. 'The answer is the distance from the earth to the sun. That's how thick it would be.'

We were enthralled by this piece of intelligence and asked him to prove it on the blackboard, which he did.

Another time, he brought a two-foot-long grass-snake into class and insisted every boy should handle it in order to cure us for ever, as he said, of a fear of snakes. This caused quite a commotion.

I cannot remember all the other thousands of splendid things that old Corkers cooked up to keep his class happy, but there was one that I shall never forget which was repeated at intervals of about three weeks throughout each term. He would be talking to us about this or that when suddenly he would stop in mid-sentence and a look of intense pain would cloud his ancient countenance. Then his head would come up and his great nose would begin to sniff the air and he would cry aloud, 'By God! This is too much! This is going too far! This is intolerable!'

We knew exactly what was coming next, but we always played along with him. 'What's the matter, sir? What's happened? Are you all right, sir? Are you feeling ill?'

Up went the great nose once again, and the head would move slowly from side to side and the nose would sniff the air delicately as though searching for a leak of gas or the smell of something burning. 'This is not to be tolerated!' he would cry. 'This is *unbearable!*'

'But what's the matter, sir?'

'I'll tell you what's the matter,' Corkers would shout. 'Somebody's *farted!*'

'Oh no, sir!' . . . 'Not me, sir!' . . . 'Nor me, sir!' . . . 'It's none of us, sir!'

Thanks awfully for the Tablets. I took some a few times and the indigestion has stopped now, they are jolly good

At this point, he would rise majestically to his feet and call out at the top of his voice, '*Use door as fan! Open all windows!*'

This was the signal for frantic activity and everyone in the class would leap to his feet. It was a well-rehearsed operation and each of us knew exactly what he had to do. Four boys would man the door and begin swinging it back and forth at great speed. The rest would start clambering about on the gigantic windows which occupied one whole wall of the room, flinging the lower ones open, using a long pole with a hook on the end to open the top ones, and leaning out to gulp the fresh air in mock distress. While this was going on, Corkers himself would march serenely out of the room, muttering, 'It's the cabbage that does it! All they give you is disgusting cabbage and Brussels sprouts and you go off like fire-crackers!' And that was the last we saw of Corkers for the day.

School dinners!

Fagging

I spent two long years as a Fag at Repton, which meant I was the servant of the studyholder in whose study I had my little desk. If the studyholder happened to be a House Boazer, so much the worse for me because Boazers were a dangerous breed. During my second term, I was unfortunate enough to be put into the study of the Head of the House, a supercilious and obnoxious seventeen-year-old called Carleton. Carleton always looked at you right down the length of his nose, and even if you were as tall as him, which I happened to be, he would tilt his head back and still manage to look at you down the length of his nose. Carleton had three Fags in his study and all of us were terrified of him, especially on Sunday mornings, because Sunday was study-cleaning time. All the Fags in all the studies had to take off their jackets, roll up their sleeves, fetch buckets and floor-cloths and get down to cleaning out their studyholder's study. And when I say cleaning out, I mean practically sterilizing the place. We scrubbed the floor and washed the windows and polished the grate and dusted the ledges

and wiped the picture-frames and carefully
tidied away all the hockey-sticks and cricket-
bats and umbrellas.

I dont think that I've told you what we do every day sort of zing: the
First bell goes at quarter-past seven, and the fag who is in water in
each bedder, gets up and fills the cans with hot water, and closes
the windows. Then if he want to, gets into bed again. The second
bell goes at half past seven, and everyone must be down for prayers
by quarter to eight. Then we l..
to an hour ....
H..

All that Sunday morning we had been slogging
away cleaning Carleton's study, and then, just
before lunch Carleton himself strode into the
room and said, 'You've had long enough.'

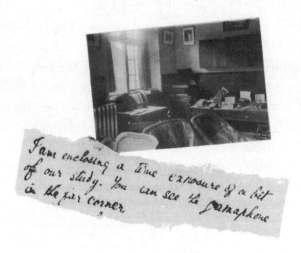

I am enclosing a time exposure of a bit
of our study. You can see the semaphone
in the fer corner.

'Yes, Carleton,' the three of us murmured, trembling. We stood back, breathless from our exertions, compelled as always to wait and watch the dreadful Carleton while he performed the ritual of inspection. First of all, he would go to the drawer of his desk and take out a pure-white cotton glove which he slid with much ceremony on to his right hand. Then, taking as much care and time as a surgeon in an operating theatre, he would move slowly round the study, running his white-gloved fingers along all the ledges, along the tops of the picture-frames, over the surfaces of the desks, and even over the bars of the fire-grate. Every few seconds, he would hold those white fingers up close to his face, searching for traces of dust, and we three Fags would stand there watching him, hardly daring to breathe, waiting for the dreaded moment when the great man would stop and shout, 'Ha! What's this I see?' A look of triumph would light up his face as he held up a white finger which had on it the tiniest smudge of grey dust, and he would stare at us with his slightly popping pale blue eyes and say, 'You haven't cleaned it, have you? You haven't bothered to clean my study properly.'

To the three of us Fags who had been slaving

away for the whole of the morning, these words were simply not true. 'We've cleaned every bit of it, Carleton,' we would answer. 'Every little bit.'

'In that case why has my finger got dust on it?' Carleton would say, tilting his head back and gazing at us down the length of his nose. 'This *is* dust, isn't it?'

We would step forward and peer at the white-gloved forefinger and at the tiny smidgin of dust that lay on it, and we would remain silent. I longed to point out to him that it was an actual impossibility to clean a much-used room to the point where no speck of dust remained, but that would have been suicide.

'Do any of you dispute the fact that this is dust?' Carleton would say, still holding up his finger. 'If I am wrong, do tell me.'

'It isn't *much* dust, Carleton.'

'I didn't ask you whether it was *much* dust or *not much* dust,' Carleton would say. 'I simply asked you whether or not it was dust. Might it, for example, be iron filings or face powder instead?'

'No, Carleton.'

'Or crushed diamonds, maybe?'

'No, Carleton.'

'Then what is it?'

'It's . . . it's dust, Carleton.'

'Thank you,' Carleton would say. 'At last you have admitted that you failed to clean my study properly. I shall therefore see all three of you in the changing-room tonight after prayers.'

The rules and rituals of fagging at Repton were so complicated that I could fill a whole book with them. A House Boazer, for example, could make any Fag in the House do his bidding. He could stand anywhere he wanted to in the building, in the corridor, in the changing-room, in the yard, and yell 'Fa-a-ag!' at the top of his voice and every Fag in the place would have to drop what he was doing and run flat out to the source of the noise. There was always a mad stampede when the call of 'Fa-a-ag!' echoed through the House because the last boy to arrive would invariably be chosen for whatever menial or unpleasant task the Boazer had in mind.

During my first term, I was in the changing-room one day just before lunch scraping the mud from the soles of my studyholder's football boots when I heard the famous shout of 'Fa-a-ag!' far away at the other end of the House. I dropped everything and ran. But I got there last, and the Boazer who had done the

shouting, a massive athlete called Wilberforce,
said, 'Dahl, come here.'

The other Fags melted away with the speed
of light and I crept forward to receive my
orders. 'Go and heat my seat in the bogs,'
Wilberforce said. 'I want it *warm*.'

You seem to have been doing a lot of printing; but when you paint the
bog, don't paint the seat, leaving it wet and sticky, or some
unfortunate person who has not noticed it, will adhere to it, and unless
his bottom is cut off *nurses in chools'* to go about with the seat
bot sticking behind him always, he will be doomed to stay where
he is

I hadn't the faintest idea what any of this
meant, but I already knew better than to ask
questions of a Boazer. I hurried away and
found a fellow Fag who told me the meaning
of this curious order. It meant that the Boazer
wished to use the lavatory but that he wanted
the seat warmed for him before he sat down.
The six House lavatories, none with doors,
were situated in an unheated outhouse and on
a cold day in winter you could get frostbite
out there if you stayed too long. This particular
day was icy-cold, and I went out through the
snow into the outhouse and entered number
one lavatory, which I knew was reserved for

Boazers only. I wiped the frost off the seat with my handkerchief, then I lowered my trousers and sat down. I was there a full fifteen minutes in the freezing cold before Wilberforce arrived on the scene.

'Have you got the ice off it?' he asked.

'Yes, Wilberforce.'

'Is it *warm*?'

'It's as warm as I can get it, Wilberforce,' I said.

'We shall soon find out,' he said. 'You can get off now.'

I got off the lavatory seat and pulled up my trousers. Wilberforce lowered his own trousers and sat down. 'Very good,' he said. 'Very good indeed.' He was like a wine-taster sampling an old claret. 'I shall put you on my list,' he added.

I stood there doing up my fly-buttons and not knowing what on earth he meant.

'Some Fags have cold bottoms,' he said, 'and some have hot ones. I only use hot-bottomed Fags to heat my bog-seat. I won't forget you.'

He didn't. From then on, all through that winter, I became Wilberforce's favourite bog-seat warmer, and I used always to keep a paperback book in the pocket of my tail-coat to while away the long bog-warming sessions. I must have read the entire works of Dickens sitting on that Boazer's bog during my first winter at Repton.

Games and Photography

It was always a surprise to me that I was good at games. It was an even greater surprise that I was exceptionally good at two of them. One of these was called fives, the other was squash-racquets.

Fives, which many of you will know nothing about, was taken seriously at Repton and we had a dozen massive glass-roofed fives courts kept always in perfect condition. We played the game of *Eton*-fives, which is always played by four people, two on each side, and basically it consists of hitting a small, hard, white, leather-covered ball with your gloved hands. The Americans have something like it which they call handball, but Eton-fives is far more complicated because the court has all manner of ledges and buttresses built into it which help to make it a subtle and crafty game.

Fives is possibly the fastest ball-game on earth, far faster than squash, and the little ball ricochets around the court at such a speed that sometimes you can hardly see it. You need a swift eye, strong wrists and a very quick pair of hands to play fives well, and it was a game I took to right from the beginning. You may find it hard to believe, but I became so good at it that I won both the junior and the senior school fives in the same year when I was fifteen. Soon I bore the splendid title 'Captain of Fives', and I would travel with my team to other schools like Shrewsbury and Uppingham to play matches. I loved it. It was a game without physical contact, and the quickness of the eye and the dancing of the feet were all that mattered.

A Captain of any game at Repton was an important person. He was the one who selected the members of the team for matches. He and only he could award 'colours' to others. He would award school 'colours' by walking up to the chosen boy after a match and shaking him by the hand and saying 'Graggers on your teamer!' These were magic words. They entitled the new teamer to all manner of privileges including a different-coloured hat-band on his straw-hat and fancy braid around the edges of his blazer and different-coloured games clothes, and all sorts of other advertisements that made the teamer gloriously conspicuous among his fellows.

A Captain of any game, whether it was football, cricket, fives or squash, had many other duties. It was he who pinned the notice on the school notice-board on match days announcing the

Fives Team Priory House

team. It was he who arranged fixtures by letter
with other schools. It was he and only he who had
it in his power to invite this master or that to play
against him and his team on certain afternoons.
All these responsibilities were given to me when
I became Captain of Fives. Then came the snag. It
was more or less taken for granted that a Captain
would be made a Boazer in recognition of his
talents – if not a School Boazer then certainly a
House Boazer. But the authorities did not like
me. I was not to be trusted. I did not like rules.
I was unpredictable. I was therefore not Boazer
material. There was no way they would agree
to make me a House Boazer, let alone a School
Boazer. Some people are born to wield power

and to exercise authority. I was not one of them. I was in full agreement with my Housemaster when he explained this to me. I would have made a rotten Boazer. I would have let down the whole principle of Boazerdom by refusing to beat the Fags. I was probably the only Captain of any game who has never become a Boazer at Repton. I was certainly the only unBoazered Double Captain, because I was also Captain of squash-racquets. And to pile glory upon glory, I was in the school football team as well.

A boy who is good at games is usually treated with great civility by the masters at an English Public School. In much the same way, the ancient Greeks revered their athletes and made statues of them in marble. Athletes were the demi-gods, the chosen few. They could perform glamorous feats beyond the reach of ordinary mortals. Even today, fine footballers and baseball players and runners and all other great sportsmen are much admired by the general public and advertisers use them to sell breakfast cereals. This never happened to me, and if you really want to know, I'm awfully glad it didn't.

But because I loved playing games, life for me at Repton was not totally without pleasure. Games-playing at school is always fun if you happen to be good at it, and it is hell if you are not. I was one of the lucky ones, and all those afternoons on the playing-fields and in the fives courts and in the squash courts made the otherwise grey and melancholy days pass a lot more quickly.

There was one other thing that gave me great pleasure at this school and that was photography. I was the only boy who practised it seriously, and it was not quite so simple a business fifty years ago as it is today. I made myself a little dark-room in a corner of the music building, and in there I loaded my glass plates and developed my negatives and enlarged them.

Our Arts Master was a shy retiring man called Arthur Norris who kept himself well apart from the rest of the staff. Arthur Norris and I became close friends and during my last year he organized an exhibition of my photographs. He gave the whole of the Art School over to this project and helped me to get my enlargements framed. The exhibition was rather a success, and masters who had hardly ever spoken to me over the past four years would come up and say things like, 'It's quite extraordinary' ... 'We didn't know we had an artist in our midst' ... 'Are they for sale?'

Arthur Norris would give me tea and cakes in his flat and would talk to me about painters like Cézanne and Manet and Matisse, and I have a feeling that it was there, having tea with the gentle soft-spoken Mr Norris in his flat on Sunday afternoons that my great love of painters and their work began.

After leaving school, I continued for a long time with photography and I became quite good at it. Today, given a 35mm camera and a built-in exposure-meter, anyone can be an expert photographer, but it was not so easy fifty years ago. I used glass plates instead of film, and each of these had to be loaded into its separate container in the dark-room before I set out to take pictures. I usually carried with me six loaded plates, which allowed me only six exposures, so that clicking the shutter even once was a serious business that had to be carefully thought out beforehand.

You may not believe it, but when I was eighteen I used to win prizes and medals from the Royal Photographic Society in London, and from other places like the Photographic Society of Holland. I even got a lovely big bronze medal from the Egyptian Photographic Society of Cairo, and I still have the photograph that won it. It is a picture of one of the so-called Seven Wonders of the World, the Arch of Ctesiphon in Iraq. This is the largest unsupported arch on earth and I took the photograph while I was training out there for the RAF in 1940. I was flying over the desert solo in an old Hawker Hart biplane and I had my camera round my neck. When I spotted the huge arch standing alone in a sea of sand, I dropped one wing and hung in my straps and let go of the stick while I took aim and clicked the shutter. It came out fine.

Goodbye School

During my last year at Repton, my mother said to me, 'Would you like to go to Oxford or Cambridge when you leave school?' In those days it was not difficult to get into either of these great universities so long as you could pay.

'No, thank you,' I said. 'I want to go straight from school to work for a company that will send me to wonderful faraway places like Africa or China.'

You must remember that there was virtually no air travel in the early 1930s. Africa was two weeks away from England by boat and it took you about five weeks to get to China. These were distant and magic lands and nobody went to them just for a holiday. You went there to work. Nowadays you can go anywhere in the world in a few hours and nothing is fabulous any more. But it was a very different matter in 1933.

So during my last term I applied for a job only to those companies that would be sure to send me abroad. They were the Shell Company (Eastern Staff), Imperial Chemicals (Eastern Staff) and a Finnish lumber company whose name I have forgotten.

I was accepted by Imperial Chemicals and by the Finnish lumber company, but for some reason I wanted most of all to get into the Shell Company. When the day came for me to go up to London for this interview, my Housemaster told me it was ridiculous for me even to try. 'The Eastern Staff of Shell are the *crème de la crème*,' he said. 'There will be at least one hundred applicants and about five vacancies. Nobody has a hope unless he's been Head of the School or Head of the House, and you aren't even a *House* Prefect!'

My Housemaster was right about the applicants. There were one hundred and seven boys waiting to be interviewed when I arrived at the Head Office of the Shell Company in London. And there were seven places to be filled. Please don't ask me how I got one of those places. I don't know myself. But get it I did, and when I told my Housemaster the good news on my return to school, he didn't congratulate me or shake me warmly by the hand. He turned away muttering, 'All I can say is I'm damned glad I don't own any shares in Shell.'

I didn't care any longer what my Housemaster thought. I was all set. I had a career. It was lovely.

got the job with Shell!

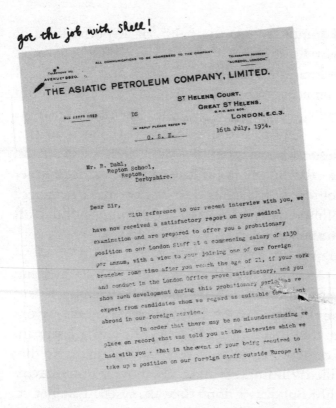

ALL COMMUNICATIONS TO BE ADDRESSED TO THE COMPANY.

TELEGRAPHIC ADDRESS
"AUREOOL, LONDON"

TELEPHONE NO.
AVENUE 9820.

THE ASIATIC PETROLEUM COMPANY, LIMITED.

St HELENS COURT,
GREAT St HELENS,
G.P.O. BOX 806.
LONDON, E.C.3.

ALL KEEPS USED

DS

IN REPLY PLEASE REFER TO

G. S. E.

16th July, 1934.

Mr. R. Dahl,
  Repton School,
    Repton,
      Derbyshire.

Dear Sir,

With reference to our recent interview with you, we have now received a satisfactory report on your medical examination and are prepared to offer you a probationary position on our London Staff at a commencing salary of £130 per annum, with a view to your joining one of our foreign branches some time after you reach the age of 21, if your work and conduct in the London Office prove satisfactory, and you show such development during this probationary period as we expect from candidates whom we regard as suitable for employment abroad in our foreign service.

In order that there may be no misunderstanding we place on record what was told you at the interview which we had with you - that in the event of your being required to take up a position on our foreign Staff outside Europe it

I was to leave school for ever in July 1934 and join the Shell Company two months later in September when I would be exactly eighteen. I was to be an Eastern Staff Trainee at a salary of five pounds a week.

That summer, for the first time in my life, I did not accompany the family to Norway.

I somehow felt the need for a special kind of last fling before I became a businessman. So while still at school during my last term, I signed up to spend August with something called 'The Public Schools' Exploring Society'. The leader of this outfit was a man who had gone with Captain Scott on his last expedition to the South Pole, and he was taking a party of senior schoolboys to explore the interior of Newfoundland during the summer holidays. It sounded like fun.

Without the slightest regret I said goodbye to Repton for ever and rode back to Kent on my motorbike. This splendid machine was a 500cc Ariel which I had bought the year before for eighteen pounds, and during my last term at Repton I kept it secretly in a garage along the Wilmington road about two miles away. On Sundays I used to walk to the garage and disguise myself in helmet, goggles, old raincoat and rubber waders and ride all over Derbyshire. It was fun to go roaring through Repton itself with nobody knowing who you were, swishing past the masters walking in the street and circling around the dangerous supercilious School Boazers out for their Sunday strolls. I tremble to think what would have happened to me had I been caught, but I wasn't caught. So on the last day of term I zoomed joyfully away and left school behind me for ever and ever. I was not quite eighteen.

I had only two days at home before I was off to Newfoundland with the Public Schools' Explorers. Our ship sailed from Liverpool at the beginning of August and took six days to reach St John's. There were about thirty boys of my own age on the expedition as well as four experienced adult leaders. But Newfoundland, as I soon found out, was not much of a country. For three weeks we trudged all over that desolate land with enormous loads on our backs. We carried tents and groundsheets and sleeping-bags and saucepans and food and axes and everything else one needs in the interior of an unmapped, uninhabitable and inhospitable country. My own load, I know, weighed exactly one hundred and fourteen pounds, and someone else always had to help me hoist the rucksack on to my back in the mornings. We lived on pemmican and lentils, and the twelve of us who went separately on what was called the Long March from the north to the south of the island and back again suffered a good deal from lack of food. I can remember very clearly how we experimented with eating boiled lichen and reindeer moss to supplement our diet. But it *was* a genuine adventure and I returned home hard and fit and ready for anything.

There followed two years of intensive training with the Shell Company in England. We were seven trainees in that year's group and each one of us was being carefully prepared to uphold the majesty of the Shell Company in one or another remote tropical country. We spent weeks at the huge Shell Haven Refinery with a special instructor who taught us all about fuel oil and diesel oil and gas oil and lubricating oil and kerosene and gasoline.

After that we spent months at the Head Office in London learning how the great company functioned from the inside. I was still living in Bexley, Kent, with my mother and three sisters, and every morning, six days a week, Saturdays included, I would dress

the Businessman

neatly in a sombre grey suit, have breakfast at seven forty-five and then, with a brown trilby on my head and a furled umbrella in my hand, I would board the eight-fifteen train to London together with a swarm of other equally sombre-suited businessmen. I found it easy to fall into their pattern. We were all very serious and dignified gents taking the train to our offices in the City of London where each of us, so we thought, was engaged in high finance and other enormously important matters. Most of my companions wore hard bowler hats, and a few like me wore soft trilbys, but not one of us on that train in the year of 1934 went bareheaded. It wasn't done. And none of us, even on the sunniest days, went without his furled umbrella. The umbrella was our badge of office. We felt naked without it. Also it was a sign of respectability. Road-menders and plumbers never went to work with umbrellas. Businessmen did.

I enjoyed it, I really did. I began to realize how simple life could be if one had a regular routine to follow with fixed hours and a fixed salary and very little original thinking to do. The life of a writer is absolute hell compared with the life of a businessman. The writer has to force himself to work. He has to make his own hours and if he doesn't go to his desk at all there is nobody to scold him. If he is a writer of fiction he lives in a world of fear. Each new day demands new ideas and he can never be sure whether he is going to come up with them or not. Two hours of writing fiction leaves this particular writer absolutely drained. For those two hours he has been miles away, he has been somewhere else, in a different place with totally different people, and the effort of swimming back into normal surroundings is very great. It is almost a shock. The writer walks out of his workroom in a daze. He wants a drink. He needs it. It happens to be a fact that nearly every writer of fiction in the world drinks more whisky than is good for him. He does it to give himself faith, hope and courage. A person is a fool to become a writer. His only compensation is absolute freedom. He has no master except his own soul, and that, I am sure, is why he does it.

The Shell Company did us proud. After twelve months at Head Office, we trainees were all sent away to various Shell branches in England to study salesmanship. I went to Somerset and spent several glorious weeks selling kerosene to old ladies in remote villages. My kerosene motor-tanker had a tap at the back and when I rolled into Shepton Mallet or Midsomer Norton or Peasedown St John or Hinton Blewett or Temple Cloud or Chew Magna or Huish Champflower, the old girls and the young maidens would hear the roar of my motor and would come out of their cottages with jugs and buckets to buy a gallon of kerosene for their lamps and their heaters. It is fun for a young man to do that sort of thing. Nobody gets a nervous breakdown or a heart attack from selling kerosene to gentle country folk from the back of a tanker in Somerset on a fine summer's day.

Then suddenly, in 1936, I was summoned back to Head Office in London. One of the

Directors wished to see me. 'We are sending you to Egypt,' he said. 'It will be a three-year tour, then six months' leave. Be ready to go in one week's time.'

'Oh, but sir!' I cried out. 'Not *Egypt*! I really don't want to go to *Egypt*!'

The great man reeled back in his chair as though I had slapped him in the face with a plate of poached eggs. 'Egypt,' he said slowly, 'is one of our finest and most important areas. We are doing you a *favour* in sending you there instead of to some mosquito-ridden place in the swamps!'

I kept silent.

'May I ask why you do not wish to go to Egypt?' he said.

I knew perfectly well why, but I didn't know how to put it. What I wanted was jungles and lions and elephants and tall coconut palms swaying on silvery beaches, and Egypt had none of that. Egypt was a desert country. It was bare and sandy and full of tombs and relics and Egyptians and I didn't fancy it at all.

'What is wrong with Egypt?' the Director asked me again.

'It's ... it's ... it's,' I stammered, 'it's too *dusty*, sir.'

The man stared at me. 'Too *what*?' he cried.

'Dusty,' I said.

'*Dusty!*' he shouted. 'Too *dusty*! I've never heard such rubbish!'

There was a long silence. I was expecting him to tell me to fetch my hat and coat and leave the building for ever. But he didn't do that. He was an awfully nice man and his name was Mr Godber. He gave a deep sigh and rubbed his hand over his eyes and said, 'Very well then, if that's the way you want it. Redfearn will go to Egypt instead of you and you will have to take the next posting that comes up, dusty or not. Do you understand?'

'Yes, sir, I realize that.'

'If the next vacancy happens to be Siberia,' he said, 'you'll have to take it.'

'I quite understand, sir,' I said. 'And thank you very much.'

Within a week Mr Godber summoned me again to his office. 'You're going to East Africa,' he said.

'Hooray!' I shouted, jumping up and down. 'That's marvellous, sir! That's wonderful! How terrific!'

The great man smiled. 'It's quite dusty there too,' he said.

'Lions!' I cried. 'And elephants and giraffes and coconuts everywhere!'

'Your boat leaves from London Docks in six days,' he said. 'You get off at Mombasa. Your salary will be five hundred pounds per annum and your tour is for three years.'

I was twenty years old. I was off to East Africa where I would walk about in khaki shorts every day and wear a topi on my head! I was ecstatic. I rushed home and told my mother. 'And I'll be gone for three years,' I said.

I was her only son and we were very close. Most mothers, faced with a situation like this, would have shown a certain amount of distress. Three years is a long time and Africa was far away. There would be no visits in between. But my mother did not allow even the tiniest bit of what she must have felt to disturb my joy.

Mama, 1936

'Oh, well done *you*!' she cried. 'It's wonderful news! And it's just where you wanted to go, isn't it!'

The whole family came down to London Docks to see me off on the boat. It was a tremendous thing in those days for a young man to be going off to Africa to work. The journey alone would take two weeks, sailing through the Bay of Biscay, past Gibraltar, across the Mediterranean, through the Suez Canal and the Red Sea, calling in at Aden and arriving finally at Mombasa. What a prospect that was! I was off to the land of palm-trees and coconuts and coral reefs and lions and elephants and deadly snakes, and a white hunter who had lived ten years in Mwanza had told me that if a black mamba bit you, you died within the hour writhing in agony and foaming at the mouth. I couldn't wait.

Although I didn't know it at the time, I was sailing away for a good deal longer than three years because the Second World War was to come along in the middle of it all. But before that happened, I got my African adventure all right. I got the roasting heat and the crocodiles and the snakes and the long safaris up-country, selling Shell oil to the men who ran the diamond mines and the sisal plantations. I learned about an extraordinary machine called a decorticator (a name I have always loved) which shredded the big leathery sisal leaves into fibre. I learned to speak Swahili and to shake the scorpions out of my mosquito boots in the mornings. I learned what it was like to get malaria and to run a temperature of 105°F for three days, and when the rainy seasons came and the water poured down in solid sheets and flooded the little dirt roads, I learned how to spend nights in the back of a stifling station-wagon with all the windows closed against marauders from the jungle. Above all, I learned how to look after myself in a way that no young person can ever do by staying in civilization.

When the big war broke out in 1939, I was in Dar es Salaam, and from there I went up to Nairobi to join the RAF. Six months later, I was a fighter pilot flying Hurricanes all round the Mediterranean. I flew in the Western Desert of Libya, in Greece, in Palestine, in Syria, in Iraq and in Egypt. I shot down some German planes and I got shot down myself, crashing in a burst of flames and crawling out and getting rescued by brave soldiers crawling on their bellies over the sand. I spent six months in hospital in Alexandria, and when I came out, I flew again.

But all that is another story. It has nothing to do with childhood or school or Gobstoppers or dead mice or Boazers or summer holidays among the islands of Norway. It is a different tale altogether, and if all goes well, I may have a shot at telling it one of these days.

*love from
BOY*

Are you wondering what happened
next to Roald Dahl?

Luckily for you here's an extract
from the second part of his story . . .

GOING SOLO

The Voyage Out

The ship that was carrying me away from England to Africa in the autumn of 1938 was called the SS *Mantola*. She was an old paint-peeling tub of 9,000 tons with a single tall funnel and a vibrating engine that rattled the tea-cups in their saucers on the dining-room table.

The voyage from the Port of London to Mombasa would take two weeks and on the way we were going to call in at Marseilles, Malta, Port Said, Suez, Port Sudan and Aden. Nowadays you can fly to Mombasa in a few hours and you stop nowhere and nothing is fabulous any more, but in 1938 a journey like that was full of stepping-stones and East Africa was a long way from home, especially if your contract with the Shell Company said that you were to stay out there for three years at a stretch. I was twenty-two when I left. I would be twenty-five before I saw my family again.

What I still remember so clearly about that voyage is the extraordinary behaviour of my fellow passengers. I had never before encountered that peculiar Empire-building breed of Englishman who spends his whole life working in distant corners of British territory. Please do not forget that in the 1930s the British Empire was still very much the British Empire, and the men and women who kept it going were a race of people that most of you have never encountered and now you never will. I consider myself very lucky to have caught a glimpse of this rare species while it

still roamed the forests and foot-hills of the earth, for today it is totally extinct. More English than the English, more Scottish than the Scots, they were the craziest bunch of humans I shall ever meet. For one thing, they spoke a language of their own. If they worked in East Africa, their sentences were sprinkled with Swahili words, and if they lived in India then all manner of dialects were intermingled. As well as this, there was a whole vocabulary of much-used words that seemed to be universal among all these people. An evening drink, for example, was always a sundowner. A drink at any other time was a chota peg. One's wife was the memsahib. To have a look at something was to have a shufti. And from that one, interestingly enough, RAF/Middle East slang for a reconnaissance plane in the last war was a shufti kite. Something of poor quality was shenzi. Supper was tiffin and so on and so forth. The Empire-builders' jargon would have filled a dictionary. All in all, it was rather wonderful for me, a conventional young lad from the suburbs, to be thrust suddenly into the middle of this pack of sinewy sunburnt gophers and their bright bony little wives, and what I liked best of all about them was their eccentricities.

It would seem that when the British live for years in a foul and sweaty climate among foreign people they maintain their sanity by allowing themselves to go slightly dotty. They cultivate bizarre habits that would never be tolerated back home, whereas in far-away Africa or in Ceylon or in India or in the Federated Malay States they could do as they liked. On the SS *Mantola* just about everybody had his or her own particular maggot in the brain, and for me it was like watching a kind of non-stop pantomime throughout the entire voyage. Let me tell you about two or three of these comedians.

I was sharing my cabin with the manager of a cotton mill in the Punjab called U. N. Savory (I could hardly believe those initials when I first saw them on his trunk) and I had the upper berth. From my pillow I could therefore look out of the port-hole clear across the lifeboat deck and over the wide blue ocean beyond. On our fourth morning at sea I happened to wake up very early. I lay in my bunk gazing idly through the port-hole and listening to the gentle snores of U. N. Savory, who lay immediately below me. Suddenly, the figure of a naked man, naked as a jungle ape, went swooshing past the port-hole and disappeared! He had come and gone in absolute silence and I lay there wondering whether perhaps I had seen a phantom or a vision or even a naked ghost.

A minute or two later the naked figure went by again!

This time I sat up sharply. I wanted to get a better look at this leafless phantom of the sunrise, so I crawled down to the foot of my bunk and stuck my head through the port-hole. The lifeboat deck was deserted. The Mediterranean was calm and milky blue and a brilliant yellow sun was just edging up over the horizon. The deck was so empty and silent that I began to wonder seriously whether I might not after all have seen a genuine apparition, the ghost perhaps of a passenger who had fallen overboard on an earlier voyage and who now spent his eternal life running above the waves and clambering back on to his lost ship.

All of a sudden, from my little spy-hole, I spotted a movement at the far end of the deck. Then a naked body materialized. But this was no ghost. It was all too solid flesh, and the man was moving swiftly over the deck between the lifeboats and the ventilators and making no sound at all as he came galloping towards me. He was short and stocky and slightly pot-bellied in his nakedness, with a big black moustache on his face, and when he was twenty yards away he caught sight of my silly head sticking out of the port-hole and he waved a hairy arm at me and called out, 'Come along, my boy! Come and join me in a canter! Blow some sea air into your lungs! Get yourself in trim! Shake off the flab!'

By his moustache alone I recognized him as Major Griffiths, a man who had told me only the night before at the dinner table how he had spent thirty-six years in India and was returning once again to Allahabad after the usual home leave.

I smiled weakly at the Major as he went prancing by, but I didn't pull back. I wanted to see him again. There was something rather admirable about the way he was galloping round and round the deck with no clothes on at all, something wonderfully innocent and unembarrassed and cheerful and friendly. And here was I, a bundle of youthful self-consciousness, gaping at him through the port-hole and disapproving quite strongly of what he was doing. But I was also envying him. I was actually jealous of his total don't-give-a-damn attitude, and I wished like mad that I myself had the guts to go out there and do the same thing. I wanted to be like him. I longed to be able to fling off my pyjamas and go scampering round the deck in the altogether and to hell with anyone who happened to see me. But not in a million years could I have done it. I waited for him to come round again.

Ah, there he was! I could see him far away down the deck, the gallant galloping Major who didn't give a fig for anybody, and I decided right then that I would say something very casual to him this time to show him I was 'one of the gang' and that I had not even noticed his nakedness.

But hang on a minute! . . . What was this? . . . There was someone with him! . . . There was another fellow scooting along beside him this time! . . . As naked as the Major he was, too! . . . What on earth was going on aboard this ship? . . . Did *all* the male passengers get up at dawn and go tearing round the deck with no clothes on? . . . Was this some Empire-building body-building ritual I didn't know about? . . . The two were coming closer now . . . My God, the second one looked like a woman! . . . It *was* a woman! . . . A naked woman as bare-bosomed as Venus de Milo . . . But there the resemblance ceased for I could see now that this scrawny white-skinned figure was none other than Mrs Major Griffiths herself . . . I froze in my port-hole and my eyes became riveted on this nude female scarecrow galloping ever so proudly alongside her bare-skinned spouse, her elbows bent and her head held high, as much as to say, 'Aren't we a jolly fine couple, the two of us, and isn't he a fine figure of a man, my husband the Major?'

'Come along there!' the Major called out to me. 'If the little memsahib can do it, so can you! Fifty times round the deck is only four miles!'

'Lovely morning,' I murmured as they went galloping by. 'Beautiful day.'

A couple of hours later, I was sitting opposite the Major and his little memsahib at breakfast in the dining-room, and the knowledge that not long ago I had seen that same little memsahib with not a stitch on her made my spine creep. I kept my head down and pretended neither of them were there.

'Ha!' the Major cried suddenly. 'Aren't you the young fellow who had his head sticking through the port-hole this morning?'

'Who, me?' I murmured, keeping my nose in the cornflakes.

'Yes, you!' the Major cried, triumphant. 'I never forget a face!'

'I . . . I was just getting a breath of air,' I mumbled.

'You were getting a darn sight more than that!' the Major cried out, grinning. 'You were getting an eyeful of the memsahib, that's what you were doing!'

The whole of our table of eight people suddenly became silent and looked in my direction. I felt my cheeks beginning to boil.

'I can't say I blame you,' the Major went on, giving his wife an enormous wink. It was his turn to be proud and gallant now. 'In fact, I don't blame you at all. Would *you* blame him?' he asked, addressing the rest of the table. 'After all, we're only young once. And, as the poet says . . .' he paused, giving the dreadful wife another colossal wink . . . 'a thing of beauty is a joy for ever.'

'Oh, do shut up, Bonzo,' the wife said, loving it.

'Back in Allahabad,' the Major said, looking at *me* now, 'I make a point of playing half-a-dozen chukkas every morning before breakfast. Can't do that on board ship, you know. So I have to get my exercise in other ways.'

I sat there wondering how one played this game of chuckers. 'Why can't you do it?' I said, desperate to change the subject.

'Why can't I do what?' the Major said.

'Play chuckers on the ship?' I said.

The Major was one of those men who chewed his porridge. He stared at me with pale-grey glassy eyes, chewing slowly. 'I hope you're not trying to tell me that you have never played polo in your life,' he said.

'Polo,' I said. 'Ah yes, of course, polo. At school we used to play it on bicycles with hockey sticks.'

The Major's stare switched suddenly to a fierce glare and he stopped chewing. He glared at me with such contempt and horror, and his face went so crimson, I thought he might be going to have a seizure.

From then on, neither the Major nor his wife would have anything to do with me. They changed their table in the dining-room and they cut me dead whenever we met on deck. I had been found guilty of a great and unforgivable crime. I had jeered, or so they thought, at the game of polo, the sacred sport of Anglo-Indians and royalty. Only a bounder would do that.

Then there was the elderly Miss Trefusis, who quite often sat at the same dining-room table as me. Miss Trefusis was all bones and grey skin, and when she walked her body was bent forward in a long curve like a boomerang. She told me she owned a small coffee farm in the highlands of Kenya and that she had known Baroness Blixen very well. I myself had read and loved both *Out of Africa* and *Seven Gothic Tales*, and I listened enthralled to everything Miss Trefusis told me about that fine writer who called herself Isak Dinesen.

'She was dotty, of course,' Miss Trefusis said. 'Like all of us who live out there, she went completely dotty in the end.'

'*You* aren't dotty,' I said.

'Oh yes, I am,' she said firmly and very seriously. 'Everyone on this ship is as dotty as a dumpling. *You* don't notice it because you're young. Young people are not watchful. They only look at themselves.'

'I saw Major Griffiths and his wife running round the deck naked the other morning,' I said.

'You call that dotty?' Miss Trefusis said with a snort. 'That's *normal*.'

'*I* didn't think so.'

'You've got a few shocks coming to you, young man, before you're very much older, you mark my words,' she said. 'People go quite barmy when they live too long in Africa. That's where you're off to, isn't it?'

'Yes,' I said.

'You'll go barmy for sure,' she said, 'like the rest of us.'

She was eating an orange at the time and I noticed suddenly that she was not eating it in the normal way. In the first place she had speared it from the fruit bowl with her fork instead of taking it in her fingers. And now, with knife and fork, she was making a series of neat incisions in the skin all around the orange. Then, very delicately, using the points of her knife and fork, she peeled the skin away in eight separate pieces, leaving the bare fruit beautifully exposed. Still using knife and fork, she separated the juicy segments and began to eat them slowly, one by one, with her fork.

'Do you always eat an orange like that?' I said.

'Of course.'

'May I ask why?'

'I never touch anything I eat with my fingers,' she said.

'Good Lord, don't you really?'

'Never. I haven't since I was twenty-two.'

'Is there a reason for that?' I asked her.

'Of course there's a reason. Fingers are filthy.'

'But you wash your hands.'

'I don't *sterilize* them,' Miss Trefusis said. 'Nor do you. They're full of bugs. Disgusting dirty things, fingers. Just think what you do with them!'

I sat there going through the things I did with my fingers.

'It doesn't bear thinking about, does it?' Miss Trefusis said. 'Fingers are just implements. They are the gardening implements of the body, the shovels and the forks. You push them into everything.'

'We seem to survive,' I said.

'Not for long you won't,' she said darkly.

I watched her eating her orange, spearing the little boats one after the other with her fork. I could have told her that the fork wasn't sterilized either, but I kept quiet.

'Toes are even worse,' she said suddenly.

'I beg your pardon?'

'They're the worst of all,' she said.

'What's wrong with toes?'

'They are the nastiest part of the human body!' she announced vehemently.

'Worse than fingers?'

'There's no comparison,' she snapped. 'Fingers are foul and filthy, but *toes*! *Toes* are reptilian and viperish! I don't wish to talk about them!'

I was getting a bit confused. 'But one doesn't eat with one's toes,' I said.

'I never said you did,' Miss Trefusis snapped.

'Then what's so awful about them?' I persisted.

'Uck!' she said. 'They are like little worms sticking out of your feet. I hate them, I hate them! I can't bear to look at them!'

'Then how do you cut your toenails?'

'I don't,' she said. 'My boy does it for me.'

I wondered why she was 'Miss' if she'd been married and had a boy of her own. Perhaps he was illegitimate.

'How old is your son?' I asked, treading carefully.

'No, no, no!' she cried. 'Don't you know *anything*? A

"boy" is one's native servant. Didn't you learn that when you read Isak Dinesen?'

'Ah yes, of course,' I said, remembering.

Absentmindedly I took an orange myself and was about to start peeling it.

'Don't,' Miss Trefusis said, shuddering. 'You'll catch something if you do that. Use your knife and fork. Go on. Try it.'

I tried it. It was rather fun. There was something satisfying about cutting the skin to just the right depth and then peeling away the segments.

'There you are,' she said. 'Well done.'

'Do you employ a lot of "boys" on your coffee farm?' I asked her.

'About fifty,' she said.

'Do they go barefoot?'

'Mine don't,' she said. 'No one works for me without shoes on. It costs me a fortune, but it's worth it.'

I liked Miss Trefusis. She was impatient, intelligent, generous and interesting. I felt she would come to my rescue at any time, whereas Major Griffiths was vapid, vulgar, arrogant and unkind, the sort of man who'd leave you to the crocodiles. He might even push you in. Both of them, of course, were completely dotty. Everyone on the ship was dotty, but none, as it turned out, was quite as dotty as my cabin companion, U. N. Savory.

The first sign of *his* dottiness was revealed to me one evening as our ship was running between Malta and Port Said. It had been a stifling hot afternoon and I was having a brief rest on my upper berth before dressing for dinner.

Dressing? Oh yes, indeed. We all dressed for dinner every single evening on board that ship. The male species of the Empire-builder, whether he is camping in the jungle or is at sea in a rowing-boat, *always* dresses for dinner, and by that I mean white shirt, black tie, dinner-jacket, black trousers and black patent-leather shoes, the full regalia, and to hell with the climate.

I lay still on my bunk with my eyes half open. Below me, U. N. Savory was getting dressed. There wasn't room in the cabin for two of us to change our clothes simultaneously, so we took it in turns to go first. It was his turn to dress first tonight. He had tied his bow-tie and now he was putting on his black dinner-jacket. I was watching him rather dreamily through half-closed eyes, and I saw him reaching into his sponge-bag and take out a small carton. He stationed himself in front of the washbasin mirror, took the lid off the carton and dipped his fingers into it. The fingers came out with a pinch of white powder or crystals, and this stuff he proceeded to sprinkle very carefully over the shoulders of his dinner-jacket. Then he replaced the lid on the carton and put it back in the sponge-bag.

Suddenly I was fully alert. What on earth was the man up to? I didn't want him to know I'd seen, so I closed my eyes and pretended to be asleep. This is a rum business, I thought. Why in the world would U. N. Savory want to sprinkle white stuff on to the shoulders of his dinner-jacket? And what *was* it, anyway? Could it be some subtle perfume or a magic aphrodisiac? I waited until he had left the cabin, then, feeling only slightly guilty, I hopped down from my bunk and opened his sponge-bag. EPSOM SALTS, it said on the little carton! And Epsom salts it was! Now what good could Epsom salts possibly do him sprinkled on his shoulders? I had always thought of him as a queer fish, a man with secrets, though I hadn't discovered what they were. Under his bunk he kept a tin trunk and a black leather case. There was nothing odd about the tin trunk, but the case puzzled me. It was roughly the size of a violin case but the lid didn't bulge as the lid of a violin case does, and it wasn't tapered. It was simply a three-foot-long rectangular leather box with two very strong brass locks on it.

'Do you play the violin?' I had once said to him.

'Don't be daft,' he had answered. 'I don't even play the gramophone.'

Perhaps it contained a sawn-off shotgun then, I told myself. It was about the right size.

I put the carton of Epsom salts back in his sponge-bag, then I took a shower, dressed and went upstairs to have a drink before dinner. There was one stool vacant at the bar so I sat down and ordered a glass of beer. There were eight sinewy sunburnt gophers including U. N. Savory sitting on high stools at the bar. The stools were screwed to the floor. The bar was semi-circular so that everyone could talk across to everyone else. U. N. Savory was sitting about five places away from me. He was drinking a gimlet, which was the Empire-builder's name for a gin with lime juice in it. I sat there listening to the small talk about pig-sticking and polo and how curry will cure constipation. I felt a total outsider. There was nothing I could contribute to the conversation so I stopped listening and concentrated on trying to solve the riddle of the Epsom salts. I glanced at U. N. Savory. From where I sat, I could actually see the tiny white crystals on his shoulders.

Then a funny thing happened.

U. N. Savory suddenly began brushing the Epsom salts off one of his shoulders with his hand. He did it ostentatiously, slapping the shoulder quite hard and saying at the same time in a rather loud voice, 'Ruddy dandruff! I'm fed up with it! Do any of you fellers know a good cure?'

'Try coconut oil,' one said.

'Bay rum and cantharides,' another said.

A tea-planter from Assam called Unsworth said, 'Take my word for it, old man, you've got to stimulate the circulation in the scalp. And the way to do that is to dunk your hair in ice-cold water every morning and keep it there for five minutes. Then dry vigorously. You've got a fine head of hair at the moment, but you'll be as bald as a coot in no time if you don't cure that dandruff. You do as I say, old man.'

U. N. Savory did indeed have a fine head of black hair, so why in the world should he have wanted to pretend he had dandruff when he hadn't?

'Thanks a lot, old man,' U. N. Savory said. 'I'll give it a go. See if it works.'

'It'll work,' Unsworth told him. 'My grandmother cured her dandruff that way.'

'Your *grandmother*?' someone said. 'Did *she* have dandruff?'

'When she combed her hair,' Unsworth said, 'it looked like it was snowing.'

For the hundredth time, I told myself that they were all totally and incurably dotty, every one of them, but I was beginning to think now that U. N. Savory might beat them all to it. I sat there staring into my beer and trying to figure out why he should go around trying to kid everyone he had dandruff. Three days later I had the answer.

It was early evening. We were moving slowly through the Suez Canal and it was hotter than ever. It was my turn to dress first for dinner. While I showered and put on my clothes, U. N. Savory lay on his bunk staring into space. 'It's all yours,' I said at last as I opened the door and went out. 'See you upstairs.'

As usual, I seated myself at the bar and began sipping a beer. By gosh, it was hot. The big slowly-revolving fan in the ceiling seemed to be blowing *steam* out of its blades. Sweat trickled down my neck and under my stiff butterfly collar. I could feel the starch in the collar going soggy around the back. The sinewy sunburnt ones around me didn't seem to notice the heat. I decided to go out on deck and smoke a pipe before dinner. It would be cooler there. I

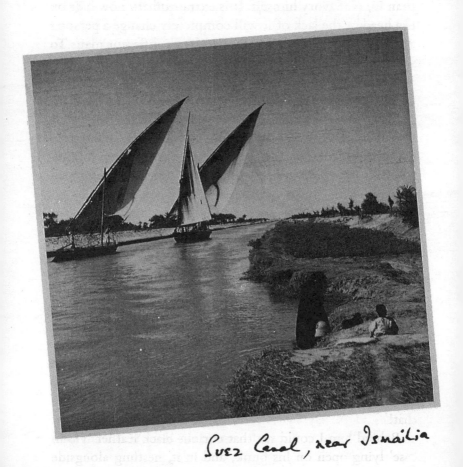

Suez Canal, near Ismailia

felt for my pipe. Damnation, I had left it behind. I stood up and made my way downstairs to the cabin and opened the door. There was a strange man sitting in shirtsleeves on U. N. Savory's bunk and as I stepped inside, the man gave a queer little yelp and jumped to his feet as though a cracker had gone off in the seat of his pants.

The stranger was totally bald and that is why it took me a second or two to realize that he was in fact none other than U. N. Savory himself. It is extraordinary how hair on the head or the lack of it will completely change a person's appearance. U. N. Savory looked like a different man. To start with, he looked fifteen years older, and in some subtle way he seemed also to have diminished, grown much shorter and smaller. As I said, he was almost totally bald, and the dome of his head was as pink and shiny as a ripe peach. He was standing up now and holding in his two hands the wig he had been about to put on as I walked in. 'You had no right to come back!' he shouted. 'You said you'd finished!' Little sparks of fury were flashing in his eyes.

'I'm . . . I'm most awfully sorry,' I stammered. 'I forgot my pipe.'

He stood there glaring at me with that dark malevolent glint in his eye and I could see little droplets of perspiration oozing out of the pores on his bald head. I felt very bad. I didn't know what to say next. 'Just let me get my pipe and I'll clear out,' I mumbled.

'Oh no you don't!' he shouted. 'You've seen it now and you're not leaving this room until you've made me a promise! You've got to promise me you won't tell a soul! Promise me that!'

Behind him I could see that curious black leather 'violin case' lying open on his bunk, and in it, nestling alongside each other like three large black hairy hedgehogs, lay three more wigs.

'There's nothing wrong with being bald,' I said.

'I didn't ask for your opinion,' he shouted. He was still very angry. 'I just want your promise.'

'I won't tell anyone,' I said. 'I give you my word.'

'And you'd better keep it,' he said.

I reached out and took hold of the pipe that was lying on my bunk. Then I began rummaging round in various places for my tobacco pouch. U. N. Savory sat down on the lower bunk. 'I suppose you think I'm crazy,' he said. Suddenly all the bark had gone out of his voice.

I said nothing. I could think of nothing to say.

'You do, don't you?' he said. 'You think I'm crazy.'

'Not at all,' I answered. 'A man can do as he likes.'

'I'll bet you think it's just vanity,' he said. 'But it's not vanity. It's nothing to do with vanity.'

'It's OK,' I said. 'Really it is.'

'It's business,' he said. 'I do it purely for business reasons. I work in Amritsar, in the Punjab. That is the homeland of the Sikhs. To a Sikh, hair is a sort of religion. A Sikh never cuts his hair. He either rolls it up on the top of his head or in a turban. A Sikh doesn't respect a bald man.'

'In that case I think it's very clever of you to wear a wig,' I said. I had to live in this cabin with U. N. Savory for several days yet and I didn't want a row. 'It's quite brilliant,' I added.

'Do you honestly think so?' he said, melting.

'It's a stroke of genius.'

'I go to a lot of trouble to convince all those Sikh wallahs it's my own hair,' he went on.

'You mean the dandruff bit?'

'You saw it, then?'

'Of course I saw it. It was brilliant.'

'It's just *one* of my little ruses,' he said. He was getting just a trifle smug now. 'No one's going to suspect me of wearing a wig if I've got dandruff, are they?'

'Certainly not. It's quite brilliant. But why bother doing it here? There aren't any Sikhs on this ship.'

'You never know,' he said darkly. 'You never can tell who might be lurking around the corner.'

The man was as potty as a pilchard.

'I see you have more than one,' I said, pointing to the black leather case.

'One's no good,' he said, 'not if you're going to do it properly like me. I always carry four, and they're all slightly different. You are forgetting that hair *grows*, old man, aren't you? Each one of these is longer than the other. I put on a longer one every week.'

'What happens after you've worn the longest one and you can't go any further?' I asked.

'Ah,' he said. 'That's the clincher.'

'I don't quite follow you.'

'I simply say, "Does anyone know of a good barber round here?" And the next day I start all over again with the shortest one.'

'But you said Sikhs didn't approve of cutting hair.'

'I only do that with Europeans,' he said.

I stared at him. The man was stark raving barmy. I felt I would go barmy myself if I went on talking to him much longer. I edged towards the door. 'I think you're amazing,' I said. 'You're quite brilliant. And don't worry about a thing. My lips are sealed.'

'Thanks, old man,' U. N. Savory said. 'Good lad.'

I flew out of the cabin and shut the door.

And that is the story of U. N. Savory.

You don't believe it?

Listen, I could hardly believe it myself as I staggered upstairs to the bar.

I kept my promise though. I told no one. Today it no longer matters. The man was at least thirty years older than me, so by now his soul is at rest and his wigs are probably being used by his nephews and nieces for playing charades.

SS *Mantola*
4 October 1938

Dear Mama,

We're now in the Red Sea, and it is *hot*. The wind is behind us and going at exactly the same speed as the boat so there is not a breath of air on board. Three times they have turned the ship round against the wind to get some air into the cabins and into the engine room. Fans merely blow hot air into your face.

The deck is strewn with a lot of limp wet things for all the world like a lot of wet towels steaming over the kitchen boiler. They just smoke cigarettes & shout, 'Boy – another iced lager.'

I don't feel the heat much – probably because I'm thin. In fact as soon as I've finished this letter I'm going off to have a vigorous game of deck tennis with another thin man – a government vet called Hammond. We play with our shirts off, throwing the coit as hard as we can – & when we have to stop for fear of drowning in our own sweat we just jump into the swimming bath.

Have **YOU** PLAYED the **FANTASTICALLY** FUN **NEW** **ROALD DAHL** apps?

www.roalddahl.com/apps

ROALD DAHL DAY

CELEBRATE

THE PHIZZ-WHIZZING

WORLD of ROALD DAHL

EVERY YEAR on

13th SEPTEMBER!

JOIN THE PARTY AT

www.roalddahl.com

STORIES ARE **GOOD** FOR **YOU.**

Roald Dahl said,
*'If you have good thoughts, they will shine
out of your face like sunbeams and you
will always look lovely.'*

We believe in doing good things.
That's why ten per cent of all Roald Dahl income*
goes to our charity partners. We have supported
causes including: specialist children's nurses, grants for
families in need, and educational outreach programmes.
Thank you for helping us to sustain this vital work.

Find out more at roalddahl.com

That's it.
The end of the book.

HERE IS
one LAST **WORD**,
invented by **Roald Dahl**
HIMSELF.
Make sure you KEEP IT SAFE.

SCRUMDIDDLYUMPTIOUS

Adjective: Something that's delicious and lovely.